AF480787

CRYPTO DECODED

CRYPTO DECODED

Casey Cavender

Published by Meriden Press
First Printing, 2026
ISBN 979-8-9946947-8-7
Disclaimer: This publication is designed to provide accurate and authoritative information in regard to the subject matter covered. It is sold with the understanding that the author and publisher are not engaged in rendering legal, investment, or other professional services. If legal advice or other expert assistance is required, the services of a competent professional should be sought.

TABLE OF CONTENTS

ACKNOWLEDGEMENTS

Holy, holy, holy, Lord God Almighty, Who was and is and is to come!
- Revelation 4:8

I want to honor and thank the Lord God Almighty who trusted me and guided me to write every word that comes forth from this book. He alone knew that you would read these words, and He alone knows that if you will but submit to His ways he will refresh and encourage you for the balance of your days.

To my beautiful wife Manda. You are an inspiration! Thank you for allowing me this season to be obedient to the call on my heart, and for believing in me even when the path wasn't clear.

To my amazing girls. Kya and Kora you are everything to me in this world. My prayer for you is that your Mom and I have guided you in the way you should go, so that when you are older you will not depart from it. Always remember who you are and who's you are!

To Jasmin Naim, my editor and unexpected mentor. Thank you for seeing the author I could become before I saw it myself. You didn't just polish my prose; you helped me find the song within the story. Your patience with me, your deep curiosity about my story, and your ability to weave narrative threads I couldn't see transformed a collection of insights into something I'm genuinely proud of. This book exists because you believed in the voice behind the words.

Preface

At 2AM, my cursor hovered over the "Sell" button while my hands shook. I wasn't analyzing charts. I was trying to outrun fear. That moment cost me more than money, it exposed the real game I'd been losing.

Welcome to Crypto Decoded and The Mind Money Method.

I'm Casey, and I'm genuinely glad you're here.

Before we dive in, there is something important I need to tell you: This isn't another crypto book. This is the missing piece in every trading course. The psychology that determines who wins, who loses, and who survives in cryptocurrency investing.

If you've ever deleted a trading app just to reinstall it three hours later, or calculated what your portfolio "would have been worth" if you'd just held, or felt your chest tighten watching red candles cascade down your screen, this book is for you.

Not because I have the answers. But because I've felt every one of those moments. And I've learned what works when knowledge isn't enough.

I know what it feels like to lose. I've watched trades drain my account because I panicked at exactly the wrong moment. I've been scammed. I've had entire accounts drained. I've invested in rug pulls that looked legitimate until they weren't.

I've made every psychological mistake you can make in crypto. And that's why this work matters to me, because I've lived the chaos most people only read about. Each mistake taught me something that technical analysis never could: the market isn't your enemy.

Your psychology is.

Here's what nobody tells you when you start investing: everyone teaches strategies, chart patterns, and blockchain fundamentals. Almost nobody teaches emotional regulation, systematic thinking, or how to make rational decisions when your stomach is in knots and your portfolio is collapsing.

You can have the best map in the world, but if your compass is broken, you'll still get lost.

That gap between technical knowledge and psychological mastery is where most crypto investors lose everything.

The Mind Money Method isn't based on my opinions or motivational speeches. It's built on 40 years of behavioral investment research from Nobel Prize-winning economists like Daniel Kahneman and Richard Thaler. Researchers who uncovered how emotion silently drives financial decision-making.

These are the same psychological frameworks that professional investors and hedge fund managers use to maintain rational thinking during market chaos. I've spent years turning this research into systems that work, applying it to crypto markets, and now I'm sharing it with you.

Over the next nine chapters, you're going to develop psychological frameworks that most investors never discover. You'll learn to recognize when your emotions are hijacking your decisions. You'll build systematic approaches that work automatically during stress. You'll develop the same long-term perspective that separates wealthy investors from those who chase every market move.

But more than that, you'll transform who you are as a decision-maker, not just in crypto, but in every area of your life where pressure and uncertainty exist.

This book won't make you a genius. It will make you unbreakable.

You'll still feel fear when markets crash. You'll still feel greed when they soar. But you'll have something more powerful than those feelings: systems that work especially when your emotions don't.

Now, let me be straight with you about something. You'll confront parts of yourself that don't like losing or being wrong and that's where your edge begins.

This isn't easy. But that's exactly why most people fail at investing, they want easy. Mastery isn't easy. It's systematic, deliberate, and transformative.

Before we begin, here's what you need to understand: cryptocurrency is high-risk. Everything I share in this book is educational. It's about developing psychological frameworks for better decision-making, not giving you financial advice.

You're responsible for your own investment decisions. Never invest more than you can afford to lose. If you need personalized financial guidance, consult a licensed financial advisor.

My job is to teach you the psychology that separates successful investors from those who lose everything. Your job is to apply these frameworks responsibly to your unique situation and risk tolerance.

You're not doing this alone. Thousands of investors, engineers, entrepreneurs, parents, and students have all discovered the same truth: when you master your mind, the market follows.

You're joining a community of people who understand that the real edge in investing isn't better information. It's better psychological discipline, applied consistently over time.

The frameworks you're about to learn will challenge how you think about money, risk, and decision-making. They'll reveal psychological patterns you didn't know you had. And they'll give you tools to build wealth systematically instead of hoping for lucky breaks.

This isn't about beating the market. It's about mastering the mind that invests in it.

You're ready for this journey. You wouldn't be here if you weren't.

Let's begin your transformation from emotional trader to psychologically integrated investor.

Welcome to The Mind Money Method.

INTRODUCTION

CRYPTO DECODED

MASTER YOUR MIND

MASTER THE MARKETS

THE PSYCHOLOGICAL EDGE BEHIND

CRYPTO'S BIGGEST SUCCESS STORIES

THE $400,000 PSYCHOLOGY LESSON

The notification hit my phone at 3:17AM like a digital sledgehammer:

"URGENT: Major exchange compromised. All withdrawals suspended indefinitely."

I stared at the glowing screen in my dark bedroom, my stomach dropping as the reality crashed down around me. Seventy percent of my cryptocurrency portfolio. Three years of careful accumulation. Countless hours of research. My financial future was trapped inside a collapsing exchange.

Again.

Hands trembling, I opened my portfolio app. The numbers that had made me feel like a genius just yesterday now mocked me from the screen. Six figures in Bitcoin, Ethereum, and carefully selected altcoins, all locked in the digital equivalent of a bank vault. Except this one was without a key.

This was not my first crypto catastrophe. In 2014, Mt. Gox had claimed my earlier investments. Then, the 2018 crash had me panic-selling at the bottom of the market. Each time, I had sworn it would never happen again. Yet here I was, watching my financial dreams evaporate in real time while frantically clicking unresponsive withdrawal buttons.

My phone buzzed. It was a message from Dave, my crypto-obsessed neighbor: "ARE YOU SEEING THIS?? IT'S OVER!!"

The market was in freefall. Bitcoin's value had plummeted by 32% in just six hours. My remaining holdings on other platforms bled like open wounds. Three years of patient accumulation gone.

Without thinking clearly, I grabbed my keys, knowing only that I needed to be with someone who would understand. Twenty minutes later, I was pounding on Charlie's door, breathless and broken.

Meet the Most Successful Crypto Investor You've Never Heard Of

Charlie isn't just another crypto success story. While everyone else rides emotional rollercoasters through bull and bear markets, Charlie moves like a chess grandmaster. He is calculated, precise, and always three moves ahead. Despite three market cycles, with three crashes that had destroyed countless investors, his wealth has grown consistently through each one.

The door opened. Charlie took one look at my face and ushered me into his study without a word.

"Everything's gone," I blurted out, collapsing into the leather cocoon of his armchair. "The exchange has locked everything down. The market's crashing. I can't do this again, Charlie."

Charlie did not immediately respond. Instead, he walked to his desk and pulled out a worn leather journal. What he said next changed everything I thought I knew about cryptocurrency investing.

"What you're experiencing isn't investment failure," he said quietly. "It's psychological hijacking. And it's exactly why 90% of people fail at cryptocurrency investing. Not once, but repeatedly."

He opened his journal to a page filled with handwritten notes dated exactly three years earlier, during the last major crash.

"This is what I was feeling during the last meltdown," he said, pointing to entries that read like my own thoughts at that moment: "Everything's finished... This time is different... I should have sold everything..."

Then he flipped the page to reveal a series of transaction records. Neat rows of buy orders. Placed at the exact moment of maximum panic.

"That sequence of decisions, made against every emotional impulse that was screaming in my brain, is now worth eight figures," he said quietly. "Not because I predicted the recovery, but because I had developed systems to make rational decisions when everyone else, including my own emotions, were making completely irrational ones."

I looked up at him, desperation giving way to curiosity. "How? How do you do that when everything inside you is screaming to run?"

Charlie's eyes held mine. "That's the only question in crypto that actually matters. Not which projects to buy, not when to enter or exit, and not which technical indicators to follow. In my view, the only sustainable edge in this market is psychological mastery. It's the ability to recognize and counter the predictable ways your own brain sabotages your investing."

The $2.3 Million Psychology Experiment

Taking a seat by his desk, Charlie reached for his laptop and pulled up a case study that would haunt me for months.

"Let me tell you about Marcus and Jim," he began. "Same neighborhood, same income, same time period. Except Marcus had everything figured out, or so he thought."

Marcus, Charlie explained, was a brilliant software engineer who had covered the walls of his home office with so many technical charts that they resembled financial wallpaper. He followed 47 crypto influencers on X (formally Twitter) had subscribed to 12 premium research services, and could explain blockchain technology, DeFi protocols, and tokenomics to anyone who would listen. His spreadsheets tracked hundreds of cryptocurrencies with mathematical precision.

Not only this, Marcus had read every book on cryptocurrency investing, attended three blockchain conferences, and spent over 1,000 hours studying market patterns. As a result, he had superior knowledge, better analytic tools, and more market information than pretty much all the other crypto investors.

So, why did he lose $400,000 in six months?

Meanwhile, his neighbor Jim, who barely understood the differences between Bitcoin and Ethereum, had made $2.3 million during the same period.

"The difference wasn't technical..." Charlie continued, his voice taking on the tone of someone sharing a profound secret, "...it was psychological."

When in 2022 Bitcoin crashed from $69,000 to $35,000, Marcus panic-sold his entire portfolio, despite all his analysis telling him the downturn was temporary. When it recovered to $50,000 two weeks later, gripped by FOMO, he bought back in at higher prices, abandoning his calm and systematic approach. When the price dropped again, fear made him sell. When meme coins started pumping, he chased quick gains. When those crashed, his revenge-trades lost him even more.

Jim, on the other hand, bought Bitcoin every month regardless of price. He ignored the volatility, never checked his portfolio during crashes, and held through boom and bust. His inferior knowledge and simple strategy destroyed Marcus's sophisticated approach.

"Marcus had superior technical knowledge but inferior psychological control," Charlie surmised. "Conversely, Jim had basic technical knowledge but superior psychological discipline. In cryptocurrency markets, psychology beats technical analysis every single time."

The 90% Problem

Charlie leaned back in his chair and delivered the insight that would reshape my entire approach to investing:

"Here's what the crypto industry doesn't want you to know: **90% of cryptocurrency losses are caused by psychological mistakes, not technical ignorance.**"

He let that sink in before continuing.

"Think about it. Information has never been more accessible. Free technical analysis is everywhere. Market data is real-time and avaiable to everyone. The best trading strategies are shared openly on YouTube and X. Yet, it's said that 90% of crypto investors still lose money.

"If information and technical knowledge were the answer, shouldn't most people be profitable by now?"

Charlie's logic was devastating.

"The problem isn't that people don't know *what* to do," Charlie continued. "It's that they can't control their emotions enough to *actually do it*. They know they should buy low and sell high, but they buy high and sell low.

They know they should dollar-cost average, but they try to time the market. They know they should hold for the long term, but they panic-sell during crashes."

He pulled out a thick folder filled with academic research, investor behavior studies, and his own detailed observations from 15 years in the markets. Selecting one entry, he began:

"Superior psychology is the ultimate competitive advantage in cryptocurrency markets. While everyone else focuses on technical analysis, blockchain technology, and market predictions, the real winners master the psychology of money, emotion, and decision-making. They understand that cryptocurrency success isn't about predicting the future, it's about controlling yourself in the present."

Why Psychology Matters More Than Ever

"Cryptocurrency markets," Charlie explained, opening his laptop to show me some volatility charts, "...are undoubtedly the most psychologically challenging investment environment in human history."

The data he pointed to was staggering. Traditional stock markets might move 2% to 5% per day. Crypto markets routinely move by 20% to 50% in just hours. A single tweet can create or destroy billions in value. Fortunes are made and lost while people sleep.

"This extreme volatility creates extreme psychological pressure," he continued. "Your fight-or-flight responses that have evolved over millions of years to help you survive physical threats, are completely overwhelmed by the modern reality of watching your net worth fluctuate by tens of thousands of dollars in real time."

Charlie showed me brain scans comparing investor neural activity during calm markets versus times of crypto volatility. The difference was shocking. During extreme volatility, you could see the rational thinking centers shut down while the emotional centers went into overdrive.

"Your brain wasn't designed for this," he said simply. "But the investors who understand and master their psychology? They thrive in this chaos. While others panic, they stay calm. While others chase trends, they stick to strategy. While others make emotional decisions, they make rational ones."

He turned to face me directly. "Ultimately, the most successful crypto investors aren't the smartest, they're the most psychologically prepared."

The Secret Psychology Research

Over the next three hours, Charlie patiently revealed the research that had transformed his approach to investing. Before becoming known as the most successful crypto investor in our circle, he had spent 15 years as a professor of behavioral psychology, studying human decision-making under stress, cognitive bias in financial markets, and the neuroscience of risk assessment.

"When I discovered Bitcoin in 2013," he explained, "I wasn't drawn to the technology at first. Rather, I was fascinated by the psychological experiment it represented."

He showed me charts comparing investor behavior patterns across different asset classes. They made clear that crypto amplifies each of the psychological and emotional mistakes that destroys wealth in traditional markets.

"I realized that cryptocurrency wasn't just a financial innovation, it was the perfect laboratory for studying human psychology under extreme conditions.

Every emotion, every cognitive bias, every psychological trap that destroys investors gets magnified by 10 in crypto markets."

Charlie had quietly applied his psychological research to build a $47 million cryptocurrency portfolio, starting with just $10,000 in 2014. But here is what made him different: Charlie was not an expert in technical analysis. He could not code smart contracts, nor did he have insider information or special market access.

What Charlie did have was superior psychology.

This meant that while other investors panicked during crashes, Charlie's systematic emotional regulation techniques kept him calm. While others FOMO-bought during pumps, Charlie stayed disciplined by using predetermined decision frameworks. While others chased the latest trends, Charlie remained committed to his long-term stratgy. While others burned out from stress, Charlie built sustainable wealth-building systems that worked automatically in the background.

"I didn't win because I was smarter," Charlie said. "I won because I understood that markets aren't moved by fundamentals or technical patterns, they're moved by human emotion, psychology, and behavior. When I entered crypto markets, I brought psychological frameworks with me that gave massive competitive advantages."

Your Complete Psychology Arsenal

Charlie opened a filing cabinet and pulled out what looked like a comprehensive training manual containing hundreds of pages of frameworks, exercises, and real-world applications.

"Over the years, I discovered that successful crypto investing requires mastery of 20 specific psychological skills," he explained. "These aren't just mindset tips or positive thinking, they're practical frameworks for decision-making, emotional regulation, stress management, and wealth building that create a measurable competitive advantage."

With these frameworks, he had quietly helped a small group of private clients to build millions in cryptocurrency wealth while avoiding the psychological traps that lay waste to most investors. Now, faced with my abject distress, Charlie was willing to share his complete crypto psychology mastery system with me.

"By the time you finish learning these frameworks," he said, "you will have complete emotional mastery over fear, greed, FOMO, and panic. Not only this, you will have systematic approaches to making optimal choices under uncertainty and pressure. And you will possess techniques for maintaining peak performance during extreme market chaos, as well as understanding risk in ways that preserve and grow wealth."

"Most importantly," Charlie continued, "you will develop psychological advantages that extend far beyond cryptocurrency into every area of your life."

Each framework was practical, immediately applicable, and designed to create measurable results. I would learn not just what to think, but how to think. Not just what to do, but how to do it consistently under pressure.

The Promise: Your Psychological Edge

As dawn broke through the windows of Charlie's study, he made me a promise that seemed impossible given my current state:

"By the end of our work together, you will make better decisions un-der pressure because you will have systematic frameworks instead of emotional reactions. You will suffer less stress during volatility because you will understand and control your psychological responses. Finally, you will build more wealth because you will avoid the psychological mistakes that destroy most portfolios."

"You will have sustainable systems that work automatically, even when markets are chaotic. You will develop competitive advantage that compounds over time and transfers to all areas of life."

Charlie leaned forward, his voice taking on an intensity I had not heard from him before.

"Most importantly, you will join the small percentage of crypto investors who succeed because they have mastered the psychology of success."

Why This Matters Right Now

"Cryptocurrency is still in its early stages," Charlie explained, backing up his points with adoption curves and market penetration data. "We're not at the end of the opportunity; oh no, we're at the beginning. But as these crypto markets mature and more institutional money enters, psychological edge will become even more important."

He was trying to tell me that the easy money phase was ending. That the time when you could buy anything and make profits was over. From now on, the biggest returns would go to investors with superior psychology, better decision-making, and stronger emotional control.

"The question isn't whether cryptocurrency will create more millionaires," Charlie told me. "It's whether you'll be one of them."

Your Journey Starts Now

As I left Charlie's house that morning, I noticed my perspective had completely shifted. The exchange hack that had devastated me hours earlier now seemed exactly the wake-up call I needed. I was not the victim of bad luck; instead, I was the victim of bad psychology.

The frameworks Charlie had described to me were not mere theory, they were practical tools used by real investors to build real wealth.

His clients had used these exact psychological systems to:

- Build seven-figure crypto portfolios, starting from modest savings

- Maintain calm and make profitable decisions during massive market crashes

- Avoid the cycles of FOMO and panic that devastate most investors

- Create sustainable wealth-building systems that work in any market condition

- Develop psychological advantages that extend far beyond cryptocurrency

These frameworks are the basis of this book, in which every chapter builds on its predecessor to create a complete psychological mastery system. Some you will be able to implement immediately. Others you will develop over months or years. All of them will give you competitive advantages that compound over time.

"To know and not to do is not yet to know" - Lao Tzu

Reading about psychology on its own will not change your results. You must practice these frameworks, implement these systems, and integrate these principles into your daily investment process. Investors who commit to the complete transformation will achieve extraordinary results. Those who just read and forget will only ever remain average.

Which will you choose?

The Real Question

As Charlie walked me to the door, he left me with one final thought:

"The question isn't whether you have the technical knowledge to succeed in crypto. The University of YouTube has made that information free and accessible to everyone.

"The question is will you develop the psychology."

The frameworks in this book will help you answer that question. They will provide the psychological tools not just to survive the chaos of cryptocurrency markets, but to thrive in it.

Your journey toward achieving a psychological edge begins on the next page. There, Charlie is waiting to share everything he has learned with you about the psychology of cryptocurrency success.

CHAPTER 1

THE CLARITY CODE

When Your Brain Betrays Your Wallet

The phone rang at 6:23AM, jolting me awake three days after my late-night meeting with Charlie. The caller ID showed a number I did not recognize and somehow, I knew this was not good news.

"Can we talk about Solana?" the panicked voice asked before I could even say hello.

It was Marcus, the brilliant engineer Charlie had told me about, the one who had lost $400,000 despite knowing more about crypto than most professionals. Somehow, he had tracked me down and was now calling my number.

"It's happening again," Marcus whimpered, his voice cracking. "I can see the pattern forming. The market's setting up for another crash, and I can't... I can't think straight. Every instinct is telling me to sell everything, but Charlie's frameworks are telling me to hold. My brain is at war with itself."

I could hear the desperation in his voice, the same desperation I had felt just days earlier when my own portfolio was collapsing. But something had changed in me since my conversation with Charlie. Where I would once have joined Marcus in his panic, now I found myself curious about what was really happening in his mind.

"What exactly are you seeing?" I asked, grabbing a notebook to capture what had the potential to become an important lesson.

"Bitcoin's down 18% in only two days. My alt portfolio is bleeding even more. Every fiber of my being is screaming 'SELL NOW!' before things get worse. But Charlie's words about psychological hijacking and emotional decision-making keep bouncing around my head."

Marcus paused, and his shaky breaths filled the silence.

Eventually he asked, "How do you tell when your brain is trying to save you from when it's trying to destroy you?"

That question would haunt me for the next three hours until I could get to Charlie's house.

The Brain That Evolution Built

(And Why It Resists Crypto)

"Marcus is experiencing something I call 'neurological warfare'," Charlie explained as I recounted the morning's phone call. "His rational mind knows what to do, but his emotional brain has declared war on his portfolio."

Charlie pulled out what looked like a medical textbook, opening it to a page showing detailed scans of investors' brains during market stress.

"Your brain has two distinct systems that make investment decisions," he began, pointing to the highlighted areas of the scans. "And they want completely different things."

According to Nobel Prize winner Daniel Kahneman's research, these systems are:

System 1: Your Ancient Survival Brain. This evolved to handle immediate physical threats, can operate in milliseconds, and is extremely sensitive to loss. It creates intense physical sensations and triggers 'RUN!' responses during market crashes and 'CHASE!' impulses during rallies.

System 2: Your Modern Analytical Brain. This evolved to conduct complex problem-solving, operates over minutes or hours, and can process multiple probabilities and scenarios. It weighs risk against reward and suggests that you 'Hold according to plan,' during crashes, or 'Take profits systematically,' during rallies.

"Here's the problem," Charlie continued, showing me investors' brain scans taken during the 2021 crypto crash. "Under extreme stress, your survival brain literally hijacks your thinking brain. Stress hormones (cortisol and adrenaline) flood your system and shut down the pre-frontal cortex."

The scans were startling. During calm market conditions, both brain regions clearly showed balanced activity. But during periods of market chaos, the emotional centers lit up like a Christmas tree, while the rational centers went almost completely dark.

"When under high degrees of stress, you're essentially trying to solve space-age problems with caveman software," Charlie said. "Marcus isn't weak or stupid, he's simply human. His 300,000-year-old survival instincts are completely overwhelmed by the modern reality of watching his net worth fluctuate by tens of thousands of dollars in real-time."

The $847,000 Phone Call

Charlie's phone buzzed. On glancing at it, his expression immediately shifted to concern.

"It's Sarah," he said. "One of my other students. She has been doing well with the psychological frameworks, but..." He answered the call. No matter how hard I tried, it was impossible not to hear how the conversation went.

"Charlie, I need help. Now." Sarah's voice was tight with controlled panic. "I'm staring at my screen and my portfolio just dropped by $847,000 in the last six hours. Everything logical tells me this is temporary, that I should hold or even buy more. But I can feel myself breaking."

I watched Charlie lean forward, immediately focused. This was no longer purely academic, it was a real-time psychological emergency.

"Sarah, how's your breathing right now?" Charlie asked calmly.

"Fast. Shallow. My chest feels tight."

"Heart rate?"

"Racing. Like I just ran a marathon."

"Thoughts?"

"Spinning. I keep calculating how much I could lose if this continues. I'm seeing scenarios where everything goes to zero. I know it's not rational, but the numbers feel so real."

From where I sat, I could see Charlie scribbling the words "textbook hijacking" in his notebook as he listened.

"Sarah, you are experiencing what we call 'amygdala override.' This means that your emotional brain has taken control of your body and is flooding it with stress chemicals. Nothing you try to think through right now will work because thinking isn't actually available to you."

"So, what do I do?" Sarah asked, her voice breaking slightly.

"We're going to use the Clarity Code." Charlie replied, opening his laptop.

The CLARITY Code: Your First Defense Against Brain Hijacking

On Charlie's screen, I could see him pulling up what looked like an emergency protocol, the kind of step-by-step framework you need at moments when your brain turns against your wallet.

"The Clarity Code isn't about suppressing emotions," Charlie explained as Sarah listened. "It's about recognizing when your emotional brain has hijacked your decision-making. It will help create space for your rational brain to come back online."

"The CLARITY Framework I'm about to teach you gives you seven specific steps to regain control when stress hijacks your brain. Each letter is an action that counteracts what's happening in your nervous system. But the Framework only works because it's built on the Clarity Code, the deeper psychological principles that explain why smart people make catastrophic decisions under pressure. The Code is the operating system; CLARITY is how you run it."

"Sarah, we're going to walk through this together right now," Charlie said. "We'll see how each letter stands for an essential part of staying calm when investing becomes stressful."

Onscreen, I could see The CLARITY Framework in large letters:

C	**CHECK:** your physical state
L	**LOCATE:** the emotional trigger
A	**ASSESS:** the real versus the perceived threat
R	**RESET:** your nervous system
I	**INVESTIGATE:** with fresh perspective
T	**TIME-LIMIT:** your decision
Y	**YIELD:** to predetermined systems

C - CHECK Your Physical State

"Sarah, I want you to mentally scan your body from head to toe and describe what you're feeling physically," Charlie instructed.

"My shoulders are completely tense. My jaw is clenched. My stomach feels like it is in knots. My hands are actually shaking a little."

"Perfect. You are having a classic fight-or-flight response. In other words, your body is preparing either to battle a saber-toothed tiger or run from it. The problem for you is that there's no tiger, just numbers on a screen."

As Charlie spoke, I shifted uncomfortably in my chair, suddenly aware of my own clenched jaw and tight shoulders, my body betraying the same stress responses he was describing. I tried to make myself invisible, grateful that Charlie, absorbed in teaching Sarah, seemed to have forgotten I was there entirely.

As they were speaking, I realized how crucial Charlie's point was. People talk about 'emotional investing,' thinking it is all about feelings. But emotions are physical and the real chemical and neurological changes they create can impair judgment, just like Marcus experienced.

"Sarah, here's what's happening in your body right now," Charlie continued. "Adrenaline is redirecting blood flow away from your prefrontal cortex, which is your thinking brain, and toward your muscles for fight or flight instead. At the same time, cortisol is impairing your memory and making it harder to access your stored knowledge and experience. Also, your heart rate is elevated, reducing your ability to think clearly."

"So, I'm literally biochemically impaired right now?" Sarah asked.

"Exactly. Which is why trying to make rational investment decisions in this state is like trying to perform surgery while drunk."

L - LOCATE the Emotional Trigger

"Now, Sarah, I want you to identify exactly what triggered this response. It was not just the portfolio drop. What specific thought or image sent you into this state?"

Sarah was quiet for a moment. "I... I was calculating how long I could maintain my lifestyle if the losses continued. I started seeing myself having to sell my house, having to tell my kids we could not afford their private school anymore. It became a vivid nightmarish scenario."

"There it is," Charlie said, pensively. "The trigger wasn't the market movement. It was the catastrophic story your brain created about what the market movement meant."

Charlie explained to Sarah that our brains are prediction machines, constantly creating stories about what might happen next. Under stress, these prediction machines go haywire, creating increasingly dramatic and unlikely scenarios.

"Your emotional brain doesn't distinguish between a real threat and an imagined one," Charlie continued. "When you pictured losing your house, your body responded as if it was actually happening."

A - ASSESS the Real versus the Perceived Threat

"OK, let's get some perspective, Sarah. What percentage of your total net worth is in crypto?"

"About 40%."

"And if crypto went to zero tomorrow, which it won't, but if it did, what would actually happen to your life?"

While Sarah paused, I could almost hear her rational brain coming back into gear.

"I'd... I would still have my house... I would still have my retirement accounts. And I would still have my business income. I might have to adjust some spending, but my kids would still go to school, we would still eat, we would still live in the same place."

"So, the actual threat to your survival is..."

"Zero!" said Sarah, confidence seeping back. "There's no actual threat to my survival."

"But the perceived threat your emotional brain created was..."

"Total catastrophe. Loss of everything."

"This is the core insight of the Clarity Code. In cryptocurrency investing, perceived threats are almost always vastly greater than actual threats. But your brain responds to perceived threats as if they're real, creating massive psychological suffering over situations that don't threaten your well-being."

R - RESET Your Nervous System

"Sarah, next we need to get your nervous system back to baseline so you can think clearly. I want you to try something that might seem silly, but it works."

Charlie then walked Sarah through a specific breathing technique designed to activate the parasympathetic nervous system, telling her body that the emergency was over.

Take a breath in for four counts, hold for seven counts, exhale for eight counts. The exhale is longer than the inhale, which signals safety to your nervous system."

"These exercises will activate your vagus nerve, which controls your rest-and-digest response. It literally changes the brain chemistry from stress mode to calm mode."

After five minutes of guided breathing, Sarah's voice had completely changed.

"Wow. I feel… clear. Like I just woke up from a really vivid nightmare."

I - INVESTIGATE with Fresh Perspective

"Now that your rational brain is back online," Charlie said, "let's investigate what's happening in the market. Sarah, what does your systematic analysis tell you about this price movement?"

"Well, Bitcoin is down 18% since yesterday, but it's still above all the major moving averages. The on-chain metrics still look healthy, no major whale selling, or at least I can't see any large-scale investor activity, in fact network activity is stable. What I do see is some accumulation from smart money addresses."

"And how does this compare to previous corrections during bull markets?"

"Let's see… It's actually pretty typical. We have seen correction of 15–25% multiple times during every bull run. So, this is nothing unusual historically."

Charlie smiled. "Notice how different that analysis sounds from the catastrophic scenarios your emotional brain was creating 10 minutes ago?"

"It's like I was seeing the same data through completely different lenses," Sarah marveled. "One lens made everything look like the world was ending. The other made it look like a normal market movement."

T - TIME-LIMIT Your Decision

"Sarah, here's a crucial principle: never make permanent investment decisions during temporary emotional states," Charlie said. "Even though you're feeling clearer now, I want you to implement a 24-hour rule."

I overheard Charlie explaining that even after using the CLARITY Framework, the neurochemical effects of stress can linger for hours. He pointed out how much better it was to make important decisions only after completely getting back to baseline.

"Write down exactly what you're considering doing right now. Seal it in an envelope. Tomorrow at this same time, open the envelope and ask yourself if you still want to make that decision."

"What if the market crashes more while I'm waiting?" Sarah asked.

"Then you'll buy at even better prices," Charlie replied. "Remember, if your analysis is correct that this is a temporary correction, waiting helps you. If your analysis is wrong and this is the start of a major bear market, 24 hours won't matter in the context of your long-term position."

Y - YIELD to Predetermined Systems

"This is the most important part of the Clarity Framework," Charlie said, his voice assuming a more serious tone. "Sarah, when you set up your investment strategy, what did you decide to do during market corrections?"

"I have systematic buy orders that activate during corrections between 15% and 20%. I'm supposed to add to positions during moments of panic, not reduce them."

"And do you still believe in the analysis that led to that strategy?"

"Yes. Actually, I believe it more than ever. During the calm investigation phase, I remembered why I'm confident in this market cycle."

"Then you should yield to your predetermined system. Not because it is guaranteed to work, but because you made that decision in a calm, rational state after careful analysis. The emotional decision you're tempted to make now was created by brain chemistry, not improved analysis."

Charlie paused to let this sink in.

He cemented the thought with: "Over the long term, predetermined systems beat emotional reactions every single time."

The Phone Call Resolution

Twenty minutes after Sarah's initial panic call had begun, she was not only calm but clearly excited about the market opportunity her earlier terror had obscured.

"I'm going to activate my systematic buying program," she said. "And Charlie, thank you. I can't believe how completely my perspective shifted just by walking through that framework."

After Sarah hung up, Charlie turned away from his screen and was visibly shocked to see me still in the room. It was as if he had forgotten me entirely. After a slightly awkward moment, he apologized, saying "You weren't supposed to hear all that. Obviously, my lessons are strictly confidential."

He went on, "Nevertheless, now you can see the power of the Clarity Code. My student went from a state of biochemical panic to systematic opportunity recognition in 20 minutes. Not because the market changed, but because she changed her relationship with her own psychology."

"Just like you, most investors experience all of this, but they lack the tools to manage it. They make permanent decisions during temporary emotional states. They turn paper losses into real losses. They destroy years of wealth building in moments of chemical-induced panic."

Marcus Calls Back

As if on cue, my phone rang. It was Marcus again.

"I don't know what just happened," he said, sounding confused but much calmer than during his morning call. "About an hour ago, something... shifted. The same market data that was terrifying me this morning suddenly looked more like an opportunity."

I smiled, knowing exactly what had happened. Marcus had unknowingly worked through his own version of the CLARITY Framework.

"What did you end up doing?" I asked.

"I bought more. For the first time in months, I bought during a dip instead of selling into it. And I feel... confident about it."

Charlie was listening and gave me a thumbs up.

"Marcus," I said, "I think you just experienced your first breakthrough in psychological investing."

The Science Behind the CLARITY Code

After Marcus had hung up, Charlie explained the neuroscience that made the CLARITY Framework so effective.

"Each step is designed to address a specific aspect of stress-induced decision-making impairment," he said, while leafing through research papers on financial decision-making under stress.

CHECK addresses the mind-body connection. Creating physical awareness interrupts automatic emotional responses.

LOCATE engages the rational brain by requiring analysis of emotional states.

ASSESS creates perspective by distinguishing real from imagined threats.

RESET uses physiology to change brain chemistry from stress to calm.

INVESTIGATE re-engages analytical thinking when the rational brain has come back online.

TIME-LIMIT prevents making decisions while stress chemistry is still lingering.

YIELD implements systematic approaches created during optimal decision-making states.

"The whole Framework takes 15 to 20 minutes to complete," Charlie said. "And in that short time, it can prevent decisions that would take months or years to recover from."

Your First Assignment: The Clarity Practice

Charlie handed me a laminated card showing the CLARITY Framework, along with specific instructions for practicing it.

"For the next week, I want you to use this before making any investment decision. I mean this not just during panic, but during excitement too," he said. "FOMO and euphoria hijack your brain just as much as fear and panic do."

Daily Clarity Practice:

- Morning: Check your emotional state before looking at markets.

- Daily: Before any trade or investment: Complete a full CLARITY assessment.

- Evening: Reflect on decisions made during different emotional states.

- Weekly: Review which emotional states led to your best and your worst decisions.

"Most people only think about psychology during crises," Charlie concluded. "But the best investors use psychological frameworks proactively, as standard operating procedure."

The Deeper Pattern

As I prepared to leave, Charlie shared one final insight that would reshape how I thought about investing psychology.

"The CLARITY Code isn't really about cryptocurrency," he said. "It's about learning to recognize when your brain is lying to you and developing tools to hear the truth instead."

"Due to a misplaced evolutionary urge, your brain will lie to you thousands of times during your investing career. It will tell you that temporary corrections are permanent disasters. It will tell you that bubbles will continue forever. It will even create vivid, terrifying scenarios that feel completely real but have almost no probability of actually happening."

"The investors who succeed long-term still experience these psychological hijackings, but they recognize them quickly and have systematic tools to respond effectively."

Charlie walked me to the door but before opening it, he paused.

"Next week, we'll talk about building emotional firewalls. You'll need more advanced systems for preventing psychological hijacking before it happens. But master the CLARITY Code first. It's the foundation everything else builds on."

The Real-World Test

That afternoon, as if the market gods wanted to test my newly acquired knowledge, Bitcoin dropped by another 12%. My phone immediately lit up with panicked messages from friends and family asking if I thought they should sell their crypto.

For the first time in my investing career, I felt... calm.

Not because I enjoyed watching my portfolio decline, but because now I had a framework for understanding what was happening in my brain in response to what was happening in the market.

I pulled out Charlie's laminated card and walked through the CLARITY Code:

CHECK: Mild tension in shoulders, elevated heart rate, but managable.
LOCATE: Triggered by seeing the red numbers, but no catastrophic story forming.
ASSESS: Portfolio down by 8% today, and by 15% from peak, which is well within normal correction range.
RESET: Three rounds of controlled breathing, tension released.
INVESTIGATE: All fundamental analysis unchanged, this looks like healthy consolidation.
TIME-LIMIT: No decisions today, reassess tomorrow with fresh perspective.
YIELD: My systematic plan calls for buying during corrections of 15% or more.

Instead of panicking, I saw only opportunity.

That evening, I bought more Bitcoin for the first time during a market dip instead of a market peak.

It felt like a small miracle.

Chapter 1 Key Takeaways

The CLARITY Code saves you from your brain's worst instincts:

1. Emotional hijacking is biochemical, not psychological weakness, during which your stress response impairs rational thinking.

2. Perceived threats are usually vastly greater than actual threats in crypto investing.

3. Never make permanent investment decisions during temporary emotional states.

4. Over the long term, predetermined systems beat emotional reactions every time.

5. The CLARITY Framework gives you the tools to recognize and interrupt psychological hijacking before it has the chance to destroy your wealth.

Your homework for this week:

- Practice the CLARITY Code before every investment decision.

- Keep a journal of your emotional states and the quality of your subsequent decisions.

- Notice the difference between decisions made during calm versus stress states.

- Use the Framework during FOMO and euphoria, not just fear and panic.

Next Lesson: How to build "Emotional Firewalls." These are advanced psychological protection systems that can prevent brain hijacking before it happens.

"Your brain will lie to you, thousands of times during your investing career. The investors who succeed long-term aren't the ones who never experience these lies, they are the ones who recognize them quickly and have systematic tools to respond effectively."

— Charlie's First Law of Crypto Psychology

CHAPTER 2

EMOTIONAL FIREWALLS

Building Psychological Defenses That Work

The Night Everything Changed

My body recognized disaster before my mind did. Heart hammering, I was reaching for my phone before the second ring. From my night-stand, the numbers 2:47AM glowed dispassionately, a series of red digits that would come back to haunt me.

Seeing Charlie's name on the screen sent ice through my veins. In six months of working together, he had never called after 9PM. His boundaries were legendary, his calmness unshakeable. If Charlie was calling now, the world was ending.

"Emergency. Turn on your computer. NOW."

He gave no further explanation. Just a command.

I stumbled to my desk, muscle memory guiding me through darkness. My trading dashboard flickered to life, and immediately I understood. Every number was red, bleeding value in real-time. Bitcoin in freefall, down 31% and accelerating. Ethereum crashing harder. My carefully constructed altcoin portfolio being methodically murdered, position by position.

The DeFi lending protocol holding 40% of my assets flashed critical warnings: *"LIQUIDATION THRESHOLD BREACHED." "MARGIN CALL IMMINENT."*

Fear turned the lining of my mouth to sand. Two years of patient building were evaporating in real time. If the protocol liquidated, everything I had built since meeting Charlie would vanish. Everything.

My finger moved toward the 'EMERGENCY LIQUIDATE' button with the inevitability of gravity. Every cell urged: ACT NOW, before this gets worse.

For a heartbeat, I wondered if I might simply not be cut out for this. Maybe some people were built for this game and others were not. Maybe I was about to find out which of the two I was.

Then Charlie's voice pierced my panic like an icicle through fever:

"Don't touch anything yet."

The 3AM Psychology Lesson

"The Singapore exchange was hacked." Charlie's insights possessed the qualities of deep water. Calm on the surface, powerful currents beneath. "Two billion drained in under an hour. Every algorithmic trading system on the planet is triggering stop-losses simultaneously. It's system-wide cascade failure."

I stared at the screen, watching my positions flash red. "Charlie, my leveraged positions... if this keeps dropping, I'll face automatic liquidation."

"Stop." The word landed as if Charlie had placed his hand on my shoulder. "Before you panic, check your liquidation threshold. You set those safety margins for exactly this moment."

My hands shook as I pulled up the details I'd configured months earlier under Charlie's careful guidance. Through the fog of panic, the math emerged in all its rational beauty: My positions wouldn't face liquidation until Bitcoin dropped another 18%. At the current rate of decline, that gave me at least 18 minutes to act, maybe more if the selling slowed.

"You have buffer room," Charlie continued. "That's enough time to think, not just react. Time to use your emotional firewall."

Even while inwardly drowning in adrenaline, I recognized what he was doing. He was teaching me in real time, under maximum pressure, when the lesson would burn deepest.

"What you're feeling," Charlie explained as my portfolio hemorrhaged, "isn't financial intuition. It's your 300,000-year-old brain software screaming 'TIGER!' at numbers on a screen. To protect you from an ancient threat, your emotional brain has declared war on your rational brain. Right now, emotion is winning."

I caught my reflection in the black screen between refreshes. The face staring back looked feral: wide eyes, clenched jaw, pure prey animal. This was far from the analytical investor I imagined myself becoming. This was a terrified ape with a trading account.

The Neuroscience of Financial Panic

"Close your eyes and scan your body," Charlie instructed, surveying me cooly. "Now, tell me what you feel."

The timing of the request seemed insane while my net worth was evaporating, but I obeyed. "Racing heart. Can't breathe properly. Chest squeezed in a vice. I'm... I'm actually sweating."

"Perfect textbook sympathetic nervous system activation. Your body is flooded with stress hormones. Adrenaline has redirected blood flow from your prefrontal cortex (your thinking brain) toward your muscles for fight or flight. Cortisol is literally impairing your memory."

On screen, Bitcoin continued its sickening descent. But something shifted in me as Charlie spoke. The symptoms remained, but a gap opened between the market's movement and my reaction to it. Instead of being pummeled by a storm, this was like watching the devastation through glass.

"This is why I studied behavioral psychology before ever touching cryptocurrency," Charlie continued. "I watched brilliant people: doctors, engineers, and professors make catastrophically stupid decisions where money was involved. Not from lack of intelligence, but because they never learned to recognize when their emotions were overtaking reason."

He paused, letting that land while my losses mounted.

"At this moment, you are experiencing neurological hijacking. Your emotional brain has taken your rational brain hostage and is demanding ransom in the form of terrible decisions."

"So, what do I do?" My voice cracked like a teenager's.

"We activate your firewall."

The Emergency Firewall Protocol

"Remember the three-layer system we designed six months ago?" Charlie's voice shifted, less teacher, more combat coordinator. "Let me remind you: Layer one: recognition; Layer two: interruption, Layer three: override. We are going live with all three."

Layer 1: Recognition - IDENTIFY THE HIJACKING

Charlie immediately took control of the situation. "First, name what's happening. Say it out loud."

I'd spent years avoiding this kind of self-examination, so the words felt foreign in my mouth: "I'm having an emotional response to a perceived survival threat."

"Good. Now, what is the actual threat if this portfolio goes to zero tonight?"

My rational brain flickered online for a moment. "I would... still have my house. My job. I would be hurt but not destroyed."

"So, the survival threat is..."

"Imaginary." The word tasted like revelation. "There's no actual threat to my survival."

Layer 2: Interruption - BREAK THE PATTERN

Without responding to my epiphany, Charlie said firmly: "Stand up. Walk to your kitchen. Don't look at the screens."

"But Charlie, the liquidation!"

"Trust the system. Let's go."

I forced myself upright, legs unsteady. Even that physical movement immediately shifted something in my nervous system, the way even a broken television can miraculously sputter back to life.

"Fill a glass with cold water. Drink slowly. Focus only on the sensation."

Standing in my kitchen at 3AM, drinking that cool water while my portfolio burned, something remarkable happened. The crushing urgency lifted, replaced by something like curiosity. I knew that in the five minutes I'd been away from the screen, my 18% buffer had likely whittled down to 13%. The fire was getting closer, yet the panic didn't return. Was this what Charlie had trained himself to feel during every crisis? This strange calm within chaos?

Layer 3: Override - SYSTEMATIC RESPONSE

"Walk back to your computer. Don't sit down yet. Find the protocol card."

I found it taped to the wall beside my monitor. It showed a decision tree we had created weeks before when my brain was still functioning. For *"Major Market Dislocation + Lending Position at Risk,"* the instructions were clear:

1.   Assess liquidation buffer (DONE)

2.   Add capital in three tranches, not panic dumps...

3.   ...only if fundamentals are unchanged (hack is external, not fundamental)

4.   Maintain a systematic approach regardless of emotional state

"The protocol says systematic injection in three stages," I said, amazed at how different this measured approach felt from my initial impulse.

"Does Singapore's hack change your fundamental analysis of the assets?"

"No. If anything, it proves why decentralization matters."

"Then execute the protocol. Exactly as written."

The Architecture of Psychological Defense

Over the next 15 minutes, Charlie guided me through the protocol while my emotional brain gradually released its death grip. Instead of panic-dumping collateral, I added three predetermined amounts at five-minute intervals. Instead of making permanent decisions based on transitory panic, I maintained systematic discipline. Instead of catastrophizing, I executed. The call ended with an agreement to pick things back up again in the morning.

By sunrise, Bitcoin had found support and had begun to recover. My positions had not only survived, they had strengthened. Tentatively jubilant, I called Charlie back.

"That," Charlie said as we watched green candles appear in pricing charts, "is what emotional firewalls feel like in action. You didn't avoid your emotions, which would be impossible and unhealthy. You prevented them from making decisions."

Dawn swept in like salvation. My portfolio had survived, but more importantly, so had I. Coffee in hand, I watched the sunrise paint my monitors gold and realized this was a fundamental step forward. That night I had not just learned to manage a crisis. I learned how to manage me.

Everyone has their version of a 3AM moment. It's the crisis that exposes the gap between who we think we are and who we really are when the world catches fire. Mine just happened to have a dollar sign attached.

Later that morning, Charlie called back to check in on me and to explain the deeper architecture behind what we had experienced during the night.

"Most investors think emotional control means suppressing feelings. That's like trying to hold your breath forever. Emotions contain valuable information. The goal isn't elimination, it's filtration."

His approach clearly borrowed from cybersecurity: Instead of blocking all traffic, you filter it. That way, valuable data can still pass through and attacks get blocked, while everything gets logged for analysis.

"Think of it as a selective membrane," Charlie continued, "letting nutrients through while blocking toxins. Your emotions are not the enemy. They are datapoints. The firewall ensures data can inform, rather than control you."

The Three-Layer Defense System

Charlie took a napkin and sketched what looked like network architecture, but for the human mind. He held the diagram where I could see it on screen and pointed out the three elements.

Layer 1: Recognition Protocols (Intrusion Detection)

- Physical monitoring: "When my shoulders rise toward my ears..."

- Mental monitoring: "When I start envisaging doomsday scenarios..."

- Behavioral monitoring: "When I check prices more often than hourly..."

These are all early warning systems for emotional hijacking.

Layer 2: Interruption Systems (Threat Containment)

- Physical breaks: Movement, breathing, sensory focus

- Mental breaks: Perspective shifts, pattern interruption

- Time breaks: Mandatory delays before major decisions

- These are potential circuit breakers for emotional spirals.

Layer 3: Rational Override (Authorized Response)

- Written protocols for different scenarios

- Decision trees that bypass emotion

- Systematic responses to chaos

These are your professional-grade rational execution systems.

"It's not about becoming emotionless," Charlie emphasized, having got to know me well these last few months. "It's about becoming emotionally intelligent. There is a universe of difference."

At that, I thanked him and ended the call, stepping away to mull how to make these ideas part of my investment strategy.

The Sarah Test Case

The next morning, I knocked on Charlie's door earlier than usual. He let me in, nodded, and gestured for me to sit while he finished a call.

Sarah's voice carried clearly from the speaker, energized, almost breathless. There was no way not to hear it.

"Charlie, something incredible happened last night! During the Singapore crash, I... I actually used the system."

"Tell me everything."

"The alerts woke me at 3AM. Urgh, it was such a shock. When I saw the numbers, that familiar panic started. You know that uncomfortable knot in your stomach? But then it was like you said, and muscle memory kicked in."

She went on with the awe of someone discovering they could fly:

"I heard myself saying out loud, 'My emotional brain is trying to make investment decisions.' Just naming it changed everything. Then I did the breathing protocol, and the movement routine. Within five minutes, I could think again."

"The most incredible part?" Sarah's voice dropped in wonder and only snippets of the rest hung in the air. "... Not emotionally easy, ... sytematically ... Like ...GPS ..."

Charlie smiled as he validated what she had said. "You just experenced automatic firewall activation. The system has integrated so deeply it triggers without conscious effort."

It was so good to see how far Sarah had come. I remembered her from our group sessions as a brilliant analyst, although seriously lacking emotional control. Six months ago, she panic-sold a fortune. Now, she was teaching me a crucial lesson through her transformation.

The Four Horsemen of Crypto Psychology

After a brief pause, I pressed Charlie for a deeper explanation of how to conquer my own emotional triggers. I could see him momentarily considering whether I was ready for the next level. Finally, he relented.

"There are four emotional patterns that destroy more portfolios than all the hacks combined," Charlie said, pulling out a series of case files. "Your firewall needs specific defenses against each one."

He called them the Four Horsemen of Crypto Psychology, and like their biblical namesakes, they brought portfolio apocalypse.

The First Horseman: FOMO

Charlie told me the story of a surgeon who built wealth for 20 years, only to lose 60% of it chasing pumps. "Fear of missing out is fear of being excluded from the tribe's success. It's older than money itself."

The defense:

1. Never buy during green candles.
2. Maintain an opportunity watchlist during calm periods.
3. Ask, "Would I buy this if it hadn't moved?" If you can't say yes,
4. you can't click buy.

The Second Horseman: FUD

"Fear, Uncertainty, Doubt. The trilogy that turns temporary dips into permanent losses." Charlie showed me charts of investors who had sold Bitcoin in 2019 at $3,000, Ethereum at $80, convinced the end had come.

The defense:

1. Distinguish sentiment from fundamentals. Has your investment thesis changed, or only the price?
2. Implement a 48-hour rule before any fear-based selling.

The Third Horseman: Confirmation Bias

Charlie's eyes grew distant. "I once held a dying project for two years because I only read positive news about it. Every warning sign showed up during what most people would call a 'bear market' falling prices, bad headlines, growing doubt, and I filtered all of it out. That omission did more than lose me money, it cost me two years of compound growth elsewhere."

The defense:

1. Actively seek bear cases.
2. Follow thoughtful critics, not just cheerleaders.
3. Conduct monthly devil's advocate sessions with yourself for every major holding.

The Fourth Horseman: Overconfidence

"The most dangerous horseman rides in after victories." Charlie advised, switching to a chart showing position sizes over time. Small during struggle, massive before catastrophe. "Success is a terrible teacher."

The defense:

1. Reduce position sizes after wins, not losses.
2. Maintain a failure journal alongside success stories.
3. Practice humility like a discipline.

Building Your Personal Defense System

Three weeks later, Marcus called me with proof that the system worked.

"Yesterday my largest altcoin dropped 45% on false rumors," he said, voice steady as stone. "The old me would have panic-sold at the bottom. This time? My firewall activated automatically."

He had recognized the hijacking, interrupted it with breathing protocols, then executed his false-rumor response plan. Not only had he not sold, he bought more. When the truth emerged about the coin, his extra position returned 30%.

"But here is the real victory," Marcus continued. "It didn't feel like willpower. It felt like engineering. Like I built something stronger than my emotions."

I was thrilled for Marcus. This was a calmer, more stable, and more successful investor, worlds away from the panic-stricken mess he had been all those weeks before.

Later, in my lesson with Charlie, I told him what great progress Marcus had made. He slowly nodded in agreement. "That's exactly right. He has learned to engineer responses that work when natural responses fail."

Charlie handed me a workbook for building personalized firewalls. "Generic advice fails because everyone's triggers are different. You'll need defenses designed for your specific psychological vulnerabilities."

The process he'd designed was meticulous:

- Map your trigger patterns

- Design personal protocols

- Create interruption mechanisms

- Build override systems

- Test during small stresses

- Refine based on results

"It's like building a custom immune system," Charlie explained, "...and no one else can build it for you."

The Information Diet

"One more thing," Charlie said, indicating some correlation data between social media usage and investment disasters. "X, Reddit, and Discord, among many others. They are designed to maximize engagement by amplifying extreme emotions. Which makes them agents of psychological warfare against rational decisions."

He then prescribed an information diet as strict as any nutrition plan:

Green Zone (Nourishing): Primary sources, whitepapers, professional analysis, your own research

Yellow Zone (Occasional): Reputable news, educational content, thoughtful market commentary

Red Zone (Toxic): Price predictions, gain / loss screenshots, 'diamond hands' pressure, anonymous tips

Looking me direct in the eye, he reinforced the message, saying: "During volatile markets, consume only green. Yellow in calm periods. Red never. It's designed to hijack your psychology for engagement."

He left, leaving that thought to sink in.

The 30-Day Integration

In my next message from Charlie, I found a challenge to build automatic defenses over the next month:

Week 1: Recognition training

1. Check your emotional state every two hours.
2. Journal every investment emotion.
3. Practice identifying hijacking without trying to change it.

Week 2: Interruption development

1. Create pattern breaks.
2. Implement waiting periods.
3. Build routines that work for your life.

Week 3: Override implementation

1. Write protocols for common patterns.
2. Practice systematic responses.
3. Test during real volatility.

Week 4: Integration and automation

1. Work toward unconscious competence.
2. Test the complete system under stress.
3. Optimize for sustainability.

"The goal," Charlie emphasized, "is making good decisions automatic, especially on the days when making good decisions feels impossible, and the system feels like it isn't working yet."

Six Months Later

When Sarah, Marcus, and I shared our results over dinner one night, they were profound:

Sarah: 47% fewer emotional trades; 23% better performance, zero panic-selling through three crashes

Marcus: 89% reduction in FOMO buys; 34% better entry timing, complete elimination of revenge trading

Me: 67% less compulsive price-checking; 45% more consistent decisions, first time ever buying during crashes instead of selling

Despite himself, Charlie was clearly pleased with our progress when I saw him next.

"The pattern is clear," Charlie observed. "You didn't stop feeling emotions. You've all built systematic tools preventing your emotions from making investment decisions."

"Emotional firewalls," Charlie concluded, "don't make you emotionless. They make you emotionally intelligent. In markets and life, that's the difference between surviving and thriving."

I thought about that night six months ago when I sat trembling over the liquidate button, drowning in my own chemistry. That person still lived inside me, but now he had a guardian. Not willpower, not discipline. Something better. A system that was stronger than feeling.

I didn't know it then, but that night was my first real test in what Charlie would later call 'the complete system.' Building a firewall was just the beginning, the first stone in a structure that would eventually reshape not just my investing, but the very way I moved through the world.

This was the night I began to build a mind that could transform chaos into opportunity, fear into data, reactions into responses. Everything that would follow, the compound advantages, the generational wealth, the ability to teach others, all traced back to that 3:17AM moment, when I learned that systematic could be stronger than emotional.

The person who called his brother for reassurance during 10% price drops was gone. In his place stood someone who could watch a crash of 50% with clinical curiosity. Not because I became emotionless, but because I became systematically responsive.

The markets would crash again. When they did, fear would come knocking. But now I had something more powerful than feelings. I had a firewall. And that made all the difference.

Chapter 2 Key Takeaways

Emotional Firewalls protect your wealth from your own psychology:

1. **Emotions contain information but should not make decisions -**The goal is intelligent filtering, not impossible suppression. Let emotions inform, not control you.

2. **Three defensive layers create systematic protection -** Recognition detects hijacking, Interruption breaks patterns, Override implements rational responses. Each layer protects when others fail.

3. **Personal customization is crucial -** Generic advice fails because everyone's psychological triggers differ. Build firewalls for your specific vulnerabilities.

4. **Social media is psychological warfare -** Strict information diets are essential. Platforms profit from your emotional volatility.

5. **Practice during calm makes perfect during chaos —** Building and testing automatic responses before you need them ensures they work when you need them most.

Your Homework

Build your personal firewall system:

-   **Complete a vulnerability assessment -** Map your emotional patterns, triggers, and historical failure points. Know your enemy (hint: it's yourself).

-   **Design custom protocols -** Create specific recognition signals, interruption techniques, and override responses for your particular psychology.

- **Implement an information diet -** Eliminate red-zone inputs immediately. Limit the yellow zone. Focus on green-zone data that nourishes your decision-making.

- **Practice daily activation -** Use small emotional episodes as training. Build automatic responses to them before large crises test you.

- **Track and refine -** Monitor what works, and what doesn't.

Your firewall should evolve with your experience.

Next Lesson: The Analysis Mindset

How to think like a professional fund manager instead of an emotional gambler.

Charlie reveals the systematic thought patterns that separate institutional investors from retail amateurs, and why cultivating superior psychology makes technical analysis 10 times more effective.

"Most investors think having emotional control means suppressing feelings. That's impossible and counterproductive. The goal isn't to eliminate emotions, it's to prevent them from making decisions for you."

- Charlie's Second Law of Crypto Psychology

CHAPTER 3

THE ANALYSIS MINDSET

*How to Think Like a Professional Fund Manager
Instead of an Emotional Gambler*

The Cost of Admission

The knock came at exactly 7:00AM, accompanied by aromas that didn't belong in my usual morning. Fresh coffee that smelled expensive and a hint of pastries that were definitely not from the corner bodega. I opened the door to find Charlie holding a tray of coffees and a leather briefcase I'd never seen before.

"Field trip," he announced with an energy that made my stomach tighten. "We're going to meet someone who will change how you think about investing forever."

Twenty minutes later we were gliding through Manhattan's financial district, buildings rising like monuments to a game I had clearly been playing all wrong. My hands were sweating despite the air conditioning. I found myself obsessively checking my reflection in the window, suddenly aware of my off-the-rack blazer among these towers filled with tailored suits.

"Where exactly are we going?" I asked as we pulled up to a building that screamed old money and new technology.

"To meet Emma," Charlie replied, his voice carrying unusual reverence. "She manages $2.8 billion in crypto assets for institutional clients. But more importantly, she's going to show you why you keep losing money."

The marble and mahogany of the lobby hit me like a slap. This wasn't my world, and it certainly didn't feature my bad habits of checking Coinbase every five minutes and scrolling crypto forums for tips. This was something else entirely. After a cordial, although mildly threatening welcome at reception, we were issued visitor badges and ushered through reinforced glass gates. Waiting in that icy vestibule for the elevator, I felt like a tourist who had accidentally wandered into a military command center.

"Charlie," I said quietly, "what if she realizes I have no idea what I'm doing?"

He smiled. "She will realize that. That's the point."

Mission Control

The elevator opened onto a floor that looked more like NASA than a trading floor. Massive displays showed data I had no chance of interpreting: heatmaps pulsed like living organisms, correlation matrices resembled abstract art, while numbers flowed in patterns I had never before encountered. The energy was wrong, too. Where was the chaos? The shouting? This felt more like a library than a trading floor.

"Charlie!" A woman in her early 40s approached with the kind of confidence that made you stand straighter. "Perfect timing. We were just finishing our morning risk assessment."

Emma's handshake was firm, professional, and somehow communicated that she had already assessed and categorized me in the three seconds it had taken her to cross the room. As she guided us to a glass-walled conference room, I caught glimpses of her team at work, calm faces making million-dollar decisions like they were ordering lunch.

The $50 Million Mirror

"So, thanks for coming in. It's great to meet you." Emma said, her attention focused more on Charlie than on me.

"Charlie and I have debated this for years," she said, settling into her chair. "Whether showing retail investors how institutions actually think helps them or just overwhelms them."

"Let's find out," Charlie replied with a slight smile.

"Before we can discuss psychology," Emma said, motioning to displays that made my home set-up look as basic as cave paintings, "I want to show you at a high level how we approach deploying capital into Bitcoin. Structure, not secrets.

The screens filled with analysis from another dimension. Whereas what I called research consisted of price charts and X sentiment, this looked like the company was planning a mission to Mars.

"OK, so walk me through your current Bitcoin analysis process," Emma asked, looking directly at me.

My face burned. "I... I look at the charts, check some news, maybe see what the analysts are saying on YouTube...."

"And then?"

"Then I decide if I think it's going up or down."

Although Emma nodded without judgment, I felt the weight of my amateur approach in her silence. "Yes, that's exactly what the vast majority of crypto investors do. And it's exactly why those investors lose their money."

She turned to the main display. "Obviously I can't give away our secrets, but this overview shows how institutional investors analyze cryptocurrency. Not because we want to predict the future, that's gambling. But to make optimal decisions in the face of uncertainty."

What I saw next made me feel like I had been playing checkers while the professionals were playing four-dimensional chess.

The Architecture of Professional Thinking

Emma walked me through their framework with the patience of someone teaching a child to read, except I was the child and my entire approach to investing needed reinvention.

"Layer One: Fundamental Analysis." Her laser pointer traced through data that meant as much to me as hieroglyphics. "We never ask, 'Will Bitcoin go up?' Instead, we ask, 'What are the probabilities of different scenarios?'"

As she explained network health metrics, developer activity, and regulatory matrices across 12 jurisdictions, I felt my amateur mindset crumbling. While I had been attempting to read price through the mists like a fortune teller, they were analyzing it like engineers studying structural integrity.

"Layer Two: Technical Analysis." The charts looked familiar until Emma overlaid them with institutional flow data, order book depth, and manipulation patterns. "Technical analysis tells you when to implement decisions that fundamental analysis has justified."

My mind suddenly filled with an image of myself the previous week, buying solely because a green candle looked convincing. The memory made me sink lower in my chair.

"Layer Three: Sentiment and Positioning." AI-powered emotion detection, institutional survey data, options flow analysis. "We buy when institutions are cautiously negative, sell when they are irrationally positive. The opposite of retail."

My X feed flashed through my mind, a whirl of all those rocket emojis I had followed into losses.

"**Layer Four: Risk Management.**" Emma's voice grew serious. "This is what separates professionals from amateurs. Before asking, 'How much can we make?' we must ask, 'How much can we afford to lose?'"

Emma confirmed that position sizing is always based on what she deemed the maximum acceptable loss. Then there was portfolio correlation analysis. Liquidity assessment. Tail risk scenarios. Every term felt like another brick in the wall between amateur me and professional them.

Real Money, Real Time

"Theory is one thing," Emma said, angling her monitor to show what looked like a training dashboard. "Let me show you how the principles work when millions are actually on the line."

A risk alert flashed red on the screen, a position worth $4.3 million had crossed some threshold. Through the glass partition, I watched the trading floor react. Or rather, not react. A trader glanced at his screen, tapped a few keys with the casual precision of someone following a checklist, then went back to his coffee. That absence of emotion unsettled me more than any market crash.

"Last week," Emma continued, "Ethereum dropped 18% overnight when European regulators released new guidance. Walk me through your response, not what you would have done a year ago, but what Charlie has taught you to do now."

I felt the familiar tightness in my chest just thinking about it. "My body would still scream to sell everything," I admitted. "But Charlie taught me to recognize that scream as the problem, not the solution. So, I would step away from the screen, activate the interruption protocol, and wait for my rational brain to come back online."

Emma nodded. "Good. You recognize the hijack. Now watch what recognizing it at scale looks like."

She pulled up an archived decision tree from that day. "Our legal team flagged the three paragraphs that actually mattered out of 200 pages of regulatory text. Comparing those against the media headlines took 15 minutes. We identified institutional support levels in 10 minutes, checked if retail had finished panic-selling in five, and calculated our position sizing in another 10."

"Forty minutes of systematic analysis before touching a $12 million position," Emma said. "We actually increased our allocation while everyone else was hitting the exit. Made 23% when the market realized the regulations were not what X thought they were."

I thought about my own process, still measured in heartbeats rather than systems. The gap between knowing Charlie's frameworks and applying them at this scale felt like standing at the edge of a canyon. I had the tools now but watching them deployed with such clinical precision showed me how far I still had to climb.

The Million-Dollar Confession

"I wasn't always so systematic," Emma said suddenly, her polished exterior cracking slightly. "Want to see something?"

She pulled up a trading history that made my stomach drop. Massive positions, wild swings, eventual destruction.

"My first year running institutional money. I turned $4 million into $900,000 in three months." Her voice carried the authority of having lived through an expensive education. "At that age, I was brilliant, analytical, and understood the technology better than anyone. Yet I traded like a gambling addict."

She pointed to specific trades. Revenge positions after losses. FOMO entries during pumps. Panic exits at bottoms. It looked exactly like my own history, just with more zeros.

"The family office I worked for almost fired me. Would have, except the patriarch had blown up his first fund the same way. He gave me one last chance to learn professional discipline."

"What changed?"

"I stopped thinking like an entrepreneur trying to hit home runs and started thinking like an engineer building systems that work in all weather."

The Five Mental Models

Emma handed me a worn notebook. It contained her original training materials, coffee-stained and margin-noted. "Five mental models separate professionals from amateurs. Master these, and the zeros in your account do not matter. The process, however, does."

"Model One: Probabilistic Thinking." She drew a branching structure on a whiteboard. "Amateurs think in binary: up or down, moon or doom. Professionals think in probability trees. Maybe a 30% chance of this, 50% chance of that. It changes everything about how you approach position sizing."

I realized I'd never once thought about probability. Every trade had been an all-or-nothing bet on a single outcome.

"Model Two: Process Over Outcome." Emma pulled up two traders' records. "Trader A made 50% last month without following a process. Trader B made 15% by following strict rules. Who is the better investor?"

"Trader A?" I ventured, already sensing I was wrong. "Watch what happens when we zoom out." Emma expanded the view from one month to a full year.

The transformation was stunning. Trader A's line looked like an EKG during a heart attack, massive spikes followed by devastating crashes. By month eight, the account showed zero. Complete blow-up.

Trader B's line climbed steadily upward like a staircase. Boring. Predictable. Profitable.

"One got lucky with a meme coin pump and thought he was a genius," Emma said. "The other built wealth systematically. In crypto, the difference between gambling and investing is whether you're still here after 12 months."

I stared at the charts, seeing my own trading history in Trader A's violent swings. How many times had I mistaken a lucky win for skill?

"Model Three: Risk-First Analysis." This hit the hardest. "All this time you've been asking: 'How much can I make?' when you should ask, 'How much can I lose?' It's like driving by only looking at the speedometer, never the road."

"Model Four: Systems Thinking." Emma showed me a series of portfolio heatmaps and correlation matrices. "You are not buying tokens. You are constructing a system. Each piece affects every other piece."

"Model Five: Contrarian Analysis." She showed sentiment indicators. "When everyone agrees, everyone is more than likely wrong. Professional money makes money by being right when consensus is wrong."

At each model, I felt as if I was uploading new software to replace my corrupted operating system.

The Transformation Protocol

"Most people think becoming professional requires complex math or inside information," Emma said, handing me an investment workbook. "In fact, the biggest difference is in psychological structure. This program will rewire your mental patterns."

I opened it to find four week-by-week transformations:

Week 1: Replace predictions with probabilities

Week 2: Document every decision process

Week 3: Analyze risk before reward

Week 4: Practice contrarian thinking

"It's like physical training," Emma explained. "You can't think your way into professional psychology. You have to exercise your way there."

Charlie added, "The first month is brutal. You will realize how emotional every decision has been. By month three, you will wonder how you ever traded any other way."

The Daily Ritual

As our session ended, Emma showed me her daily routine. Not the complex analysis, of course, which was still a black box to me, but the disciplined structure that enabled it.

"I spend 15 minutes every morning reviewing predetermined plans. I don't react to overnight moves." She showed me laminated checklists, worn at the corners from use. "Then I need 10 minutes at midday to review alerts, not prices. These are alerts for specific conditions.

Finally, there are 20 minutes after close to document decisions and update my analysis."

"That's it?"

"Discipline isn't about hours. It's about consistency. Amateur traders check prices constantly but never their process. Professionals check their process constantly and prices occasionally."

The simplicity was devastating. I had been doing everything backward.

The Great Divide

As we prepared to leave, I made one last request. "Can you show me the difference on an actual position? My analysis versus yours?"

Emma pulled up the daily Solana chart. "Tell me what you see."

"It's up 40% from recent lows. Strong momentum. Probably heading higher. Good buy?"

Emma nodded, then overlaid her analysis. The same chart transformed into something three-dimensional, with the trend now inflected by support levels, volume analysis, institutional flows, correlation data, and risk metrics.

"I see a retest of resistance with declining volume, options flow suggesting institutional distribution, the correlation with risk assets is weakening, and entry points 20% lower offering better risk-reward."

The gap between our worldviews felt infinite. But then she added something that changed everything.

"Remember that trader you passed on the way in? Six months ago, he saw exactly what you see now. The difference isn't intelligence or information. It's trained perception. And training just takes time and discipline."

The Descent

The elevator ride down felt like returning from another planet. Charlie stayed quiet, letting me process. It wasn't until we reached the street that the full weight of what I'd seen hit me.

"I've been such an... amateur," I said, the words tasting bitter but necessary.

"Everyone starts there," Charlie replied. "The question is whether you stay there."

Three hours ago, I walked into that building thinking I knew how to invest. Now, I was leaving with a very uncomfortable truth. What I then called investing had actually been gambling with a spreadsheet. Every "analysis" had just been an emotional reaction dressed in technical clothes.

But I was also leaving with something else, a blueprint for transformation. Emma did not show me a better investment strategy. She showed me a better way of thinking. The question was whether I had the discipline to take that model and rebuild my mental operating system from scratch.

"That feeling in your chest?" Charlie said with frightening insight as we reached his car. "That mix of shame and excitement. That's what the beginning of real change feels like."

He was right. Everything I thought I knew had just been demolished. But somehow, standing in the ruins of my amateurish mindset, I could see the foundation of something better. Something professional. Something that worked.

It turns out the cost of admission to professional returns is not money, it's transformation. And for the first time ever, I was willing to pay it.

Chapter 3 Key Takeaways

The Analysis Mindset transforms you from gambler to professional:

1. **Think probabilistically, not in binary options** - Assign probabilities to multiple scenarios instead of betting everything on one outcome. This changes how you think about position sizing and risk management, as well as your emotional stability.

2. **Focus on process over outcomes** - Good process with bad short-term results beats bad process with good luck. Track process quality, not just profit and loss.

3. **Risk-first analysis prevents catastrophic losses** - Ask "What can I afford to lose?" before "What can I gain?" Size your positions based on acceptable loss, not hoped-for profit.

4. **Systematic processes beat emotional reactions** - Checklists and frameworks support you when emotions fail. Build them when calm, execute them when stressed.

5. **Professional investing psychology is trainable** - The gap between amateur and professional is not intelligence, it is trained perception and disciplined structure. Both can be developed systematically.

Your Homework

Begin your transformation from amateur to professional with these disciplines:

- **Shift from Predictions to Scenario Planning** – Stop asking, "Will Bitcoin hit $100,000?" and start asking, "What are the likely scenarios?" Define a Bull, Bear, and Base case.

- **Example:** You might decide there's a 60% chance of a slow climb to $90,000 (Base), 20% chance of a breakout above $100,000 (Bull), and 20% chance of a correction below $70,000 (Bear). Even if these weights are based on your observations rather than hard data, the act of assigning them prevents **outcome bias** and ensures you have a plan for the 20% chance that things go wrong.

- **Create systematic checklists** - Build decision frameworks for entries, exits, and position sizing. Use them religiously, especially when emotions run high.

- **Start every analysis with risk assessment** - Before calculating potential gains, determine your maximum acceptable loss and select positions accordingly.

- **Practice contrarian thinking** - When everyone agrees, ask why they might be wrong. Find the overlooked risk in euphoria, the hidden opportunity in despair.

- **Document your process** - Record not just what you decided but why. Review this weekly to identify how your emotional-patterns may be corrupting your analysis.

Next Lesson: The Long-Term Edge

How to build sustainable wealth systems that compound psychological advantages over time.

Charlie will reveal why thinking in terms of decades instead of days creates the ultimate competitive advantage in cryptocurrency markets, and why patience pays better than prediction.

"The biggest difference between professional and amateur investors is not intelligence or information access, it is psychological structure. Amateurs think like gamblers hoping to get lucky. Professionals think like engineers by building systems that work over time."

- Emma's First Law of Professional Investing Psychology

CHAPTER 4

THE LONG-TERM EDGE

*How to Build Sustainable Wealth Systems That
Compound Psychological Advantages*

The Summons

The letter arrived on a Tuesday morning, delivered by courier and in an envelope so thick it felt like holding money itself. My name had been handwritten with a fountain pen on the front, in the kind of deliberate script that suggested the author was someone who measured time differently than I did.

Inside was a piece of cream-colored card that read:

"You are cordially invited to the annual gathering of The Decade Covenant, a private collective of individuals committed to building generational wealth through patient capital. Your recent work with Charlie has earned you consideration for membership. Saturday, 2PM, location enclosed. Attendance is invitation-only. Silence is the threshold."

My hands trembled slightly as I read the message twice more. The address led to an estate 40 miles north, in the hills where tech billionaires build compounds away from the valley's endless noise and prying eyes.

When I showed Charlie the invitation, something shifted in his usually composed face. Pride mixed with something deeper... almost reverence.

"The Decade Covenant," he said quietly, setting the letter down like it might shatter. "I started advocating for your seat shortly after our training started."

"What exactly is it?" I asked, not fully grasping the weight of what I held.

"Twelve individuals who've each built eight- or nine-figure crypto portfolios by thinking in decades, not days."

He studied me with fresh eyes. "They don't invite traders. They invite people who understand that time is the ultimate edge."

My stomach tightened. "Charlie, I've only been at this for 18 months. My longest hold is maybe... a year?"

"They see something in you," he said. "The question is whether you're ready to see it in yourself."

The Ascent

Saturday arrived with the kind of crisp autumn air that made everything feel significant. Today, it seemed, would be different. The drive north took me through progressively more exclusive neighborhoods until GPS led me onto a private road marked only by a discrete bronze plaque: "Private Property. No Access."

My aging Honda felt increasingly inadequate as the road wound higher. Security cameras tracked my progress toward a gatehouse that looked like it could withstand a siege. Its ominous appearance did little to calm my nerves. There, a guard checked my name against a list before waving me through with directions to "the Library."

Parking between a Bentley and a Tesla Roadster, my imposter syndrome just would not be suppressed. What was I doing here? These people had forgotten more about acquiring wealth than I had ever learned. Maybe I should leave now. Say I got sick.

"First time?"

A woman in her 50s stood by the entrance, her smile suggesting she had witnessed this exact crisis before. Everything about her, from the understated Patek Philippe around her wrist to the way she stood, whispered old money learned young.

"That obvious?" I managed.

"The pause in the parking lot gives it away," she said breezily, extending her hand. "Victoria. I manage a family office focused on digital assets. $400 million under management."

Four hundred million. I managed not to choke as we shook hands.

"And don't worry," she added with surprising warmth, "I remember my first gathering. I threw up in the boxwood hedges from nerves. Come on, they're waiting."

The Council of Titans

The Library could have been airlifted from an English manor house. It had floor-to-ceiling books, Persian rugs thick enough to muffle secrets, and chairs arranged in a perfect circle as if for a meeting of some ancient council. Eleven people awaited us, each radiating the calm that comes from never checking prices.

A twelfth chair sat empty. Charlie moved toward it with the ease of someone returning home, and suddenly I understood. He wasn't just my mentor, he was one of them. For a year and a half, he'd been preparing me for this moment from the inside.

"Welcome," said a man with silver hair and eyes that had clearly seen multiple market cycles. "I'm Robert. We understand you have been working with Charlie on psychological mastery."

As the introductions proceeded, my sense of inadequacy deepened. A former Medallion Fund quant. An investor who had participated in the original Ethereum genesis, someone who held the first blocks ever mined. A behavioral economist who had authored the papers I was studying. Each had discovered cryptocurrency, not as speculation, but as inevitable technological evolution.

When my turn came, my voice cracked slightly. "I'm... I am still learing. Transitioned from panic-trading to systematic investing about eight months ago. Built a modest six-figure portfolio. Nothing compared to..." I gestured weakly at the room.

"Six figures built systematically beats eight figures lucky," said a younger member named David. "We've all been where you are. The question is, where are you going?"

Robert leaned forward. "Before we continue, answer me honestly: What's the longest you have ever held a losing position?"

The question landed like a punch. "I... maybe three months? Usually, I cut my losses much faster."

Someone to my left chuckled. "He's honest, at least."

"Three months," Robert repeated, kindly. "We measure in decades here. Are you prepared for that kind of temporal shift?"

My face burned. "I want to be. I'm just not sure I know how."

"That," Robert said, surprising me with a smile, "is the perfect answer."

The 20-Year Mirror

Victoria activated a massive display that charted Bitcoin's history from genesis block to the present, then extending 20 years into the future. But this was not the usual price chart that dominated my daily existence. This was something else entirely.

"Most people see this," she said, clicking forward to a standard pricing chart in which the violent peaks and valleys mimicked the frantic, jagged spikes of a panicked heart. "We see this." Another click transformed the same data into an assemblage of adoption curves, network effects, and institutional integration timelines that extended decades into the future.

"Internet adoption took 25 years to reach maturity," Victoria continued. "Mobile phones, 20 years. Credit cards, 30 years. Major technological transformations happen on generational timescales."

The chart showed cryptocurrency at roughly 4% global adoption. From this perspective, it was sharply evident that we were not in the late stage of a speculation bubble. We were in the prologue to a decades-long transformation.

"When you understand you are investing in a 20-year monetary revolution, rather than a single trade, daily price movements become what?" Victoria asked, looking directly at me.

"Noise," I heard myself say, Charlie's voice resounding inside my head. "Just... noise."

"Wonderful. Now you are beginning to see."

Dr. Sarah Lin, the behavioral economist, stood up next. "The human brain is completely unprepared for decade-scale thinking. Evolution optimized us for immediate threats, not patient wealth building." As she spoke, she showed brain scans that I craned toward to see clearly.

"Short-term investors show massive limbic activation during volatility." she went on, indicating the bright colors. "Their emotional brains are constantly on fire. Long-term investors?" She clicked to a different scan. "You can clearly see their minimal limbic response. Enhanced prefrontal activity. These groups are essentially using different brains."

"But here's the key," she said, eyes finding mine. "This isn't genetic. It is trained. Which is why you are here."

Perhaps on a different day I might have found this news exciting. Thrilling even. Right then, however, all I could conjure was fear.

The Test

Robert got to his feet, moving to a nearby whiteboard with the deliberation of someone about to reveal sacred knowledge. "We have a tradition here. Potential new members must demonstrate their understanding of long-term thinking to join our group. Not intellectually, that is. Anyone can parrot concepts. I mean viscerally."

My mouth went dry. This was it. The test I had no way of foreseeing.

"Tell us," Robert said, "about your biggest investment regret. Not your biggest loss, but your biggest failure of long-term thinking."

The room waited. I could lie, minimize, deflect. But looking at these faces, people who had mastered the very thing I failed at time after time, only truth would do.

"March 2020," I began, voice thick with shame. "COVID crash. I owned Bitcoin at $8,000. Watched it fall below $4,000. My portfolio dropped by 50% in days. Intellectually, I knew that nothing fundamental had changed. Bitcoin didn't care about viruses or pandemics. But I sold. All of it. At the bottom." This was not a great moment to realize I had never really processed my feelings about all the losses.

I forced myself to continue. "Bitcoin went to $61,000 within a year. If I had held, if I had bought more, I would have made life-changing wealth. Instead, I panic-sold for a $30,000 loss and watched from the sidelines as more patient investors got rich."

The silence stretched out. Then Victoria asked quietly, "What would you do differently today?"

"I wouldn't just hold," I said, surprising myself with my certainty. "I would buy more. Systematically. Every week of the crash. Because the technology did not change. The adoption curve did not change. Only the price changed. And price..."

"...is noise," the room said in unison.

Robert nodded slowly. "Pain is the best teacher. The question is whether you have truly learned."

The Initiation

"Close your eyes," Dr. Lin instructed. "We are going to show you something most people never see... Your future self."

I expected some simple visualization. What happened instead felt more like time travel.

"You are 65 years old. You have held your core crypto positions for 20 years, through four major cycles, dozens of crashes, endless volatility. While others traded in and out, you accumulated. While others panicked, you planned. Now, open your future eyes. What do you see?"

The vision hit with surprising clarity. Not supercars or yachts, those were trader dreams. I saw freedom. A modest but beautiful home, paid in full. My children educated without debt. My time completely my own. Not rich like a lottery winner, but with the true wealth of someone who had built something real over time.

"Now," Dr. Lin s voice cut through, "let's see what happens if you fail. If you keep thinking in months instead of decades. This time you have chased every pump, panicked at every dump. Open those eyes."

This vision hurt. Still working at 65. Still checking prices obsessively. Still hoping for a big score that never comes. The same financial anxiety, just with gray hair and aching limbs.

"The difference between those futures," Dr. Lin said as I opened my eyes to find the room watching me intently, "is the decision you make right now. Today. At this moment."

The Michael Revelation

Robert pulled out a worn folder. "Let me tell you about Michael. A teacher from Ohio. He started buying Bitcoin in 2013 with $500 per month from his salary. Had no special knowledge. No trading skills. No insider information."

The simple spreadsheets showed $500 invested monthly, regardless of price. Through the 2014 crash. Through the 2017 bubble and 2018 collapse. Through COVID. Through everything.

"Total invested over 12 years: $72,000. Current value: $12.7 million."

The number hung in the air like an accusation. While I thought I'd been clever, analyzing, trading, winning and losing, a teacher with a basic strategy had built generational wealth through pure patience.

"Show him your calculation," Victoria said gently.

Robert pulled up another spreadsheet. "If you had held that COVID-era Bitcoin or better yet, bought monthly since then, where would you be?"

The numbers made me dizzy. Mid-seven figures. From a mid-five figure starting point.

"This isn't about making you feel bad," Robert said. "It's about bringing home the cost of short-term thinking. Really feeling it. Because until that pain exceeds the pain of being patient, you will keep making the same mistakes."

I felt tears threaten the corners of my eyes, embarrassing but unstoppable. All those clever trades. All that analysis. All that activity. And a teacher with nothing but a calendar and discipline had destroyed my returns by doing absolutely nothing, except buying and holding.

The Council's Decision

"We need to discuss our findings," Robert announced. "Please wait in the garden."

I found myself on a terrace overlooking hills that rolled toward the ocean. The late afternoon sun painted everything gold. My phone buzzed with crypto alerts that I didn't check, they were suddenly messages from a different lifetime.

Forty minutes passed. I alternated between hope and the certainty they would reject me. Why would these titans want an amateur who panic-sold at the bottom?

Victoria appeared. "They are ready for you."

We slowly walked toward my judgment, the air weighing heavy around me. The council sat as before, but the arrangement had slightly shifted. A space had opened in their circle.

Robert stood to face me. "We have debated. Some members think you are too green, too reactive, too new to truly commit to decade-long thinking."

My heart sank.

"But" he continued, "others of us see something else. Someone who admits their mistakes. Who feels the cost of impatience. Who's still young enough to build true long-term wealth, assuming you start now."

He paused, while the room held its breath with me.

"The vote was close. Seven to four. Robert, as the convener, had abstained, but the majority was enough. He smiled. "Welcome to the Decade Covenant."

The relief hit so hard I swayed. Victoria steadied me with a gentle hand on my shoulder.

"The invitation comes with commitments, however," Robert contiued. "There must be minimum 10-year holding periods. No trading on volatility. Systematic accumulation regardless of market conditions. Annual sharing of insights with this group. Can you commit to that?"

"Yes." The word came out fierce, certain. "I have paid enough in tuition fees to short-term thinking."

"Then let's begin your real education."

The True Architecture

What followed were four hours of the most profound financial education of my life. Not tips or strategies, but the blueprints for building wealth across decades. Even my most in-depth lessons with Charlie couldn't come close.

They showed me their own portfolios. Not the holdings, which of course varied. But the structure, the thinking, the time horizons that made daily volatility imperceptible.

"Layer One: Digital Store of Value." Robert explained. "Starting with 40% in Bitcoin. Not because it's going up next month, although it might, but because monetary systems take decades to transform, and we are in year 12 of a 40-year shift."

"Layer Two: Platform Infrastructure." David took over. "That means

30% in Ethereum and competing smart contract platforms. The internet of value needs infrastructure. We are investing in digital railways, not train tickets."

"Layer Three: Innovation Capture." This was Victoria's specialty. "Place 20% in emerging sectors like DeFi, AI integration, real-world assets. Higher risk but with asymmetric returns. Some will go to zero. One might go up by a multiple of 1,000."

"Layer Four: Optionality." The youngest member, Marcus, managed this strategy. "Reserve 10% for cash and hedges. Not for trading, but for opportunities. When others are forced to sell, we are positioned to buy."

But it was the discussion about time that changed me. They showed holding periods, positions opened in 2013 that were still untouched. 2017 buys still accumulating. Even purchases made in 2021 with 80% drawdowns, still held without flinching.

"We don't have diamond hands," Robert explained. "We have decade eyes. Once you see it in decades, holding through downturns is not hard. It's logical."

The Transformation

As sunset approached, something fundamental had shifted. The person who had entered this beautiful estate checking prices every hour was now a stranger. In his place sat someone who understood that wealth was not built in moments of drama but in patient decades.

"You feel it," Dr. Lin observed. "The temporal shift. Like putting on glasses after years of squinting."

She was right. Everything looked different with decade vision. The daily volatility that had consumed me now quietened. The patient accumulation I had dismissed as boring and unrewarding revealed itself as the only strategy that worked.

"One final thing," Robert said as we prepared to leave. He handed me a small leather journal. "Michael's first investment diary. The Ohio teacher. He gave it to us with his blessing when he retired at the age of 50. Nobody understands better than a teacher how to share knowledge to help others learn. Read in his own words how an ordinary person built extraordinary wealth through nothing more sophisticated than patience."

I opened it to the first entry: *"Bought 0.5 Bitcoin today for $105. Wife thinks I am crazy. Maybe I am. But the internet changed everything in only 20 years. Maybe magic internet money will too. Will buy more next month regardless of price."*

"That thinking," Robert said, "built more wealth than all of the day traders combined. My question is: Can you think like that?"

The Descent

I sat in my car for 20 minutes before driving away, afraid that movement might break the spell. When I eventually did start the engine, driving felt unreal, as if I'd never sat behind a wheel before. In my rearview mirror, the estate grew smaller, but what had happened inside expanded with each breath.

My phone buzzed insistently while I navigated the steep downhill bends. Price alerts. Telegram signals. Discord notifications. The entire apparatus of short-term financial thinking was demanding my attetion.

I turned it off completely for the first time in three years.

The drive home took an hour, but I was already thinking in decades.

The person who panic-sold countless positions, who chased every pump, who confused movement with progress was still there, but shrinking like a shadow at noon.

At a red light, I did some quick math. Say I put $500 monthly into Bitcoin and Ethereum. For twenty years, through whatever came. No selling. No trading. No clever optimizations. Just time and mathematics working their patient magic.

The light turned green. I glided toward a future that finally made sense.

That night, Charlie called. "How do you feel?"

"Like I have been trying to sprint a marathon all this time," I said. "And just learned how to walk."

"Perfect," he replied. "Now you are ready to build real wealth. Not by doing more, you understand, but by doing less, for longer, than anyone else is willing."

I opened Michael's journal reverentially. Twelve years of entries. Same strategy every month, no matter what. While I had been spinning plates, he had been building wealth. The simplicity was beautiful. His results were undeniable.

My own journal's first entry wrote itself that night: "Committed to decade thinking today. Will buy $500 monthly regardless of price. Future self will thank present self. The wait begins."

And for the first time in my investing life, waiting felt like winning.

Chapter 4 Key Takeaways

1. **The Long-Term Edge** creates sustainable wealth through psychological mastery:

2. **Think in decades, not days** - Cryptocurrency is a 20-year technological transformation, not a trading opportunity. Daily prices are noise; adoption curves are signal.

3. **Separate technology from price** - The Covenant members built wealth by ignoring daily volatility and focusing on decade-long conviction. Price noise becomes irrelevant when you think in geological time.

4. **Build systems, not positions** - Systematic accumulation beats price prediction. Structure beats speculation. Time beats timing.

5. **Train patience like a skill** - Long-term thinking is not natural but it is trainable. Use visualization, reframing, and community support to develop decade vision.

6. **Feel the cost of impatience** - Calculate what short-term thinking has cost you. Let that pain drive your transformation. Your biggest losses contain your most important lessons.

Your Homework

Begin your journey from trader to investor:

- **Calculate your actual cost** - What would your portfolio be worth if you had simply held over the same period? Explore your deepest feelings about this number.

- **Write your decade thesis** - Document why crypto matters in 2035, not next month. Focus on adoption, not price.

- **Start systematic accumulation** - Choose an amount you can invest monthly 10 years. Begin immediately. Ignore price.

- **Visualize both futures** - See yourself at 65, both with and without patience. Which future will you choose?

- **Join the long-term community** - Find others committed to decade thinking. Short-term thinkers will sabotage your patience.

- **Delete pricing apps** - Check monthly, not hourly. What matters in decades does not change in minutes.

Next Lesson: Risk Mastery

How to think about downside protection like institutional investors instead of gambling addicts...

Charlie reveals why proper risk management is the ultimate source of long-term advantage, and how to build robust portfolios that get stronger during crises.

"Most crypto investors remain psychological adolescents, seeking immediate gratification, reacting to short-term events. Decade-scale thinking requires psychological maturity. The wait is the wealth."

- Robert's Law of Generational Wealth

CHAPTER 5

RISK MASTERY

*How to Think About Downside Protection Like an
Institutional Investor Instead of a Gambling Addict*

The Night Everything Vanished

The call came at 11:47PM on a Thursday, jolting me from sleep with an urgency that could only signal catastrophe. The number was unfamiliar, but the panicked voice on the other end was someone I had met briefly at one of Charlie's workshops.

"Everything's gone," the voice gasped between what sounded like muffled sobs. "Two years of savings. My kids' college fund. The down payment for our house. All of it... just gone."

I sat up in bed, instantly alert. "Simon, is that you? What happened?"

Simon was a software engineer who had seemed incredibly thoughtful about crypto investing when we'd met. Unlike most retail investors, he read white papers, understood the technology, and had what appeared to be a systematic approach to building his portfolio. He was using part of his salary each month to construct a future for his family.

"Leverage," he whispered, as if saying the word louder might make his situation worse. "I was so confident in my analysis. Bitcoin, Ethereum, Solana. I knew they were all going up in the long term. The leverage was supposed to accelerate my gains, not... not destroy everything."

The story poured out in fragments. Simon had been building his crypto portfolio systematically for two years, carefully following many of the psychological principles for controlling fear we had been learning with Charlie. But three months ago, watching his positions steadily appreciate, he felt invincible. The psychology that protected him from losses hadn't prepared him for the intoxication of winning and he made what seemed at the time like a rational decision to use leverage. Why not optimize his returns, he asked himself? He'd borrowed against his holdings to buy more crypto, multiplying both his potential gains and his potential losses.

"The math made perfect sense," Simon said, his voice hollow with disbelief. "75% loan-to-value ratio, borrowing against my crypto without overextending. I limited it to Bitcoin and Ethereum, kept cash aside for margin calls if prices dipped. I calculated every scenario, except..."

"Except what?"

"Except the one that actually happened. A coordinated liquidation cascade that dropped Bitcoin by 35% in four hours. My margin got called. The liquidation algorithms sold everything at the bottom. Two years of patient accumulation wiped out in a single night. What am I going to tell my family?"

As Simon's story unfolded, I realized I was witnessing the difference between understanding risk intellectually and managing it psychologically. Simon had done the math, but he had not mastered the psychology of risk, and that had cost him everything.

"Look, I hope it's ok to tell you all this...," Simon continued. " Charlie gave me your number. He said if ever this happened, you would know what to do. But I don't think there's anything you or anyone else can do now."

I looked at the clock: 11:52PM. The time was irrelevant. I knew Charlie would want to hear about this immediately.

The 3AM Risk Masterclass

Charlie answered at the first ring, as if he had been expecting the call.

"Simon's leverage position got liquidated in a flash crash," I said quietly. "Everything's gone. He's devastated."

"Is he safe? I mean, physically and emotionally safe?"

"Shaken but stable. More in shock than panic at this point."

"Good. Tell him to come over immediately. You, too. It's time for the lesson I hoped none of my students would ever need. It might be the most important thing he ever learns about wealth building."

Twenty minutes later, the three of us were sitting in Charlie's study.

As he recounted his story in more detail, Charlie and I listened silently to this masterclass in how psychological errors can destroy even the most careful mathematical calculations.

"Simon," Charlie said when the story was complete, "you have just received the most expensive education in risk management any student of mine has ever had. The question is whether you are going to learn from it or let it destroy your relationship with wealth building forever."

Charlie pulled out what looked like a medical textbook, which naturally fell open to a chapter on trauma psychology. The neural storms in the brain scans on the page raged in epic meteorological confrontations.

"Financial loss has the potential to cause real trauma," he explained, tracing his finger across the contours of the colorful images. "Your brain is processing this the same way it would a physical attack or life-threatening event. The neural pathways being formed right now will influence your relationship with money and investing for decades."

He turned to a page containing the brain scans of people who had experienced a range of traumatic events. The patterns were eerily similar whether the trauma was due to physical assault, natural disaster, or catastrophic financial loss.

He explained, "This is why most people who experience catastrophic financial losses never recover psychologically. The trauma creates such powerful fear associations in them that they become incapable of taking even the measured risks necessary to build wealth. They become victims of financial PTSD, flinching at every market movement, paralyzed by the memory of that one devastating night."

Simon looked up, his eyes still hollow but showing the first flicker of curiosity. "So how would a person recover from something like this?"

"By understanding that what happened to you wasn't only down to bad luck or market manipulation," Charlie replied. "Yes, the event happened. But your experience was a case of the predictable psychological failure that thousands of investors experience every year in the face of these events. And more importantly, it's completely preventable with proper risk-management psychological thinking."

The Brain Under Siege

Charlie moved to his whiteboard and began to sketch a vague cross-section of the human brain. His drawings were crude but effective, showing two distinct areas lighting up in different colors.

"The human brain has two completely different systems for evaluating risk," he explained, "and they are constantly at war during every investment decision you make."

He pointed to the lower part of the brain near where it meets the spine. "This is your ancient risk system, centered in the amygdala and limbic system. It evolved to keep your ancestors alive when a rustling bush might hide a dangerous predator. It can mobilize in milliseconds, causing you to feel fear and flooding your body with adrenaline before your conscious mind even knows what's happening."

Charlie drew arrows that indicated how signals travel from this ancient system. "This system is extremely sensitive to potential losses. It can't calculate probabilities or expected values. It only knows one thing: threat equals run, hide, or freeze.

When you see your portfolio dropping, this is what screams at you to sell everything and hide under your bed."

He then motioned to the front section of the brain diagram. "But here's your modern risk system in the prefrontal cortex. This evolved much later, giving us the ability to plan, analyze, and make complex decisions. It can weigh probabilities, consider multiple scenarios, and make calculated trade-offs between risk and reward."

"So, why didn't my modern system save me last night?" Simon asked, leaning forward despite his exhaustion.

Charlie's marker squeaked across the whiteboard as he drew thick arrows from the ancient system that overwhelmed the modern one.

"Because under extreme stress, like watching your life savings evaporate in real-time, your ancient system completely hijacks any other control mechanism. It's like trying to do calculus while being chased by a bear. The same neural pathways that would have saved your ancestor from a saber-toothed tiger took over to protect you from financial danger by shutting down your ability to think rationally."

I watched Simon's face as Charlie calmly explained this neuroscience. For the first time since his liquidation, understanding began to replace the confusion.

"What you're saying is, I literally couldn't think straight?" Simon asked.

Charlie nodded. "Your rational brain would have been screaming the right answers at you, maybe telling you to add to positions at these discounts, certainly not to sell at the bottom. But your survival brain had already grabbed the wheel. Under extreme financial stress, you lose access to rational thinking entirely. You become as helpless as our ancestors facing a predator, except nowadays, the predator is a red number on a screen."

To illustrate, Charlie showed us the brain scans of real investors that had been recorded during margin calls. Their rational thinking centers (the areas we would need to make good decisions) had gone completely dark, while the emotional centers lit up like flares in the night sky.

It was no different to watching a city lose power block by block until only the emergency back-up systems remained.

"This is why leverage can be so psychologically dangerous," Charlie continued. "It's not just the mathematical risk of amplified losses. It's that leverage creates the exact conditions that shut down your ability to think clearly when you need that ability most."

The Hierarchy of Survival

Charlie opened his laptop and pulled up risk management frameworks that had been produced by major institutions. "You need to start by understanding that professional investors don't think about risk the way retail investors do," he explained. "They start with a completely different question. Amateurs ask, 'What could I gain?' Professionals ask, 'What could I lose, and if I do, how will I survive it?'"

He showed us a pyramid structure. It looked simple enough. Deceptively simple.

"Think of risk as having a hierarchy as rigid as military command," Charlie explained. "At the foundation lies Level 1, or what we call survival risk. It's basically the cardinal sin of risking the money you need to live or continue investing. This is like a poker player betting their rent money. Even if they win, the decision was catastrophically stupid because losing would have destroyed their ability to keep playing."

Simon winced. His leveraged bet had clearly violated this foundational principle.

Charlie continued, moving up the pyramid. "Above survival risk sits Level 2, opportunity risk. This is more subtle but equally dangerous. It's when poor positioning prevents you from capitalizing on the times when markets gift you incredible discounts. Imagine having all your capital locked up in losing positions when Bitcoin drops to prices you know are absurdly cheap. You can see the opportunity of a lifetime, but you can't act on it."

"That's exactly what happened to me," Simon said quietly. "I knew Bitcoin at those crash prices would have been an incredible opportunity, but my margin calls meant I was forced to sell instead of buy."

"Exactly. You were forced to do the opposite of what every fiber of your analytical mind knew was right." Charlie moved to the top of the pyramid. "Only in Level 3 at the peak do we find optimization risk. These are the calculated bets that accelerate wealth building without threatening your foundation. This is where the professionals operate, taking intelligent risks for asymmetric rewards, but only after ensuring their survival and opportunity are protected. They have to. It's not just their own money and reputations riding on it, but the assets of all their clients as well."

"Your leverage strategy," Charlie said, turning to Simon, "Was simply Level 1 survival risk disguised as Level 3 optimization. You thought you were accelerating your returns when in fact you were playing Russian roulette with your entire future."

Watching the exchange, I realized that most investors, myself included, skirted our own invisible landmines of psychological risk, we just had not stepped on ours yet. How many of us were one margin call away from Simon's fate?

The Psychology of Intelligent Risk-Taking

"Most people think risk management is the same as risk avoidance," Charlie continued, pulling out research papers written by behavioral finance luminaries. "But that's like thinking physical fitness comes from never lifting anything heavy. Intelligent risk-taking is the foundation of all wealth building. The question is how to take risks that will compound wealth instead of destroying it."

He spread out an array of studies comparing successful versus unsuccessful investor patterns.

"Look at what these papers tell us unsuccessful investors do," Charlie said, highlighting key passages. "Here we see evidence of taking major risks for small potential gains, day trading with their life savings to make just 2%, using leverage to juice returns from 15% to 20%. They are risking everything to gain virtually nothing."

Simon nodded painfully. His leverage was an attempt to turn a potential 50% annual return into 75%. It was hardly worth losing everything.

"But here's what's really interesting," Charlie continued. "These same investors avoid small risks that offer massive potential gains. They will not put $1,000 into an early-stage investment that could return a multiple of 100 because they might lose it all, but they will risk $100,000 on leverage that might gain them an extra 20%. The rationale is completely backwards."

Next, Charlie showed us portfolio data from leading institutional investors. "Professional investors do the opposite. Here you can see them taking many small risks for potentially large gains, which is what we call asymmetric opportunity. They are comfortable losing small amounts frequently because they know one big winner will pay for all the losses. But they never take large risks, even for large potential gains, because they understand that staying in the game is more important than any single opportunity."

"You could say it's like the difference between a professional poker player and a gambling addict," I offered.

"Exactly!" Charlie said. "The professional knows that individual hands of cards don't matter. What matters is playing thousands of hands, backed by proper bankroll management. The gambler goes all-in on suited connectors because, this time, it might really be the big one."

The psychological difference was becoming clear. Successful investors had trained themselves to feel comfortable being wrong frequently as long as they were right about the big things. They might make 50 small investments whereby 40 of them lose money, but the 10 that work return 10x or even 100x.

Conversely, unsuccessful investors need to be right frequently, so they make concentrated bets on what they think are sure things, but that destroy them when they are wrong about the one big thing that matters.

Rebuilding the Investor's Mind

Charlie handed Simon a leather-bound workbook that was well-worn from use. "This framework has helped dozens of my students rebuild portfolios after catastrophic losses. But you have to commit to following it exactly, even when it feels overly conservative."

He opened the book to the first section, where the pages were organized like a recovery program, divided into clear phases and milestones.

"Recovery from financial trauma follows predictable stages," Charlie began. "The crux is that, just like physical therapy after an injury, you can't skip steps or rush the process without risking re-injury."

Phase One: Psychological Recovery (Months 1–3)

"The first three months are about psychological recovery. Your emotional brain will still be in full activation mode, flooding you with stress hormones every time you even think about investing. During this phase, complete abstinence from leverage, options, futures, or any form of amplified risk is non-negotiable."

Simon looked uncomfortable. "You're saying I need therapy for losing money?"

"Therapy for trauma," Charlie corrected firmly. "Your brain doesn't distinguish between financial catastrophe and physical threat. The treatment is the same because the neurological impact is the same."

"During this phase," he continued, "you will limit yourself to low-risk assets: Treasury Bills, high-yield savings, maybe some stable value funds. The goal is not about making returns. It's to rebuild your confidence so that you can make financial decisions without catastrophic outcomes."

Phase Two: Conservative Re-entry (Months 4–12)

"Months four through 12 represent conservative re-entry to investing with risk management. Think of it like learning to walk again. Maximum 2% position sizes for any individual investment. Every decision requires a written risk analysis. This should include the answers to: What could go wrong? How would you handle it? What is the maximum you are willing to lose?"

Charlie showed us the "Investor Recovery Workbook" his other students had used. They looked like pre-flight checklists, methodically working through every aspect of risk before committing capital. While the full system was designed for professional-grade execution, the core logic was simple: discipline over emotion.

"As you can see, by using this template you are retraining your brain to think systematically about risk rather than emotionally. Each small success rebuilds neural pathways that reinforce confidence. Each managed loss proves you can handle setbacks without catastrophe."

Phase Three: Advanced Risk Management (Year 2 and beyond)

"Only by year two and beyond do you earn the right to take intelligent risks again. By then, you will have rebuilt your psychological infrastructure. You should be able to look at a 30% drawdown without your amygdala hijacking your rational mind. There will be no more panic. Market crashes should seem like opportunities rather than threats."

"Most importantly," Charlie concluded, "you will never again confuse gambling with investing."

From Fear to Antifragility

"The ultimate goal," Charlie went on, pulling up model portfolios on his laptop screen, "is building what Nassim Nicholas Taleb would call an 'antifragile' portfolio. What you want is one that actually strengthens during periods of crisis, rather than weaker."

He showed us portfolio construction principles used by the most sophisticated institutional investors. Even at a glance we could see the design was elegantly simple.

"Picture your portfolio as a barbell," Charlie said, heaving a small barbell out from behind his desk to demonstrate. "At one end, you load 80–90% of your wealth into boring, stable assets that would survive a nuclear winter.

For crypto investors, this might be Bitcoin and Ethereum positions you've built through years of patient accumulation, never traded, never leveraged, just steadily growing through compound appreciation."

He lifted one end of the barbell with a touch of mock drama. "This end is heavy, stable, boring. It's not sexy. You are not bragging about it on social media. But just having it ensures you can survive anything the market might throw at you."

Pointing to the other end, he smiled. "But here's where it gets interesting. That remaining 10–20% becomes your very own venture capital fund. From this, you can spread minor bets across moonshot opportunities, new protocols, emerging technologies, and contrarian positions. Each investment from this bucket is sized to go to zero without affecting your lifestyle or psychology."

"The key insight," Charlie said, setting the barbell on his desk, "is that there should be nothing in the middle. No medium-risk, medium-return investments. You are either protecting wealth or swinging for the fences, never caught in the deadly middle because that's where leverage destroyed Simon's dreams."

Simon studied the model carefully. "So, are you saying I would have been fine if I'd just put 10% into leveraged positions instead of leveraging my entire portfolio?"

"Not quite," Charlie corrected him. "Leverage is almost never appropriate for individual investors because it violates the antifragile principle. Your barbell approach would be to place 80% of the portfolio in solid holdings and 20% in high-risk, high-reward protocol investments but never leveraged. If you do that, each small bet can go to zero, but any one of them could also return 50x or 100x. Meanwhile, your core 80% is ticking over nicely."

Charlie pulled up examples from real portfolios. "Your safe allocation might comprise 40% Bitcoin and 40% Ethereum, that you've accumulated systematically over time. Never sold, never traded, just growing.

Your speculative 20% might be spread across twenty different positions: early-stage DeFi protocols, emerging Layer 1s, gaming tokens, whatever has asymmetric potential."

"Each position is 1% of your portfolio. If they all go to zero, you will have lost 20%. However, if just one returns 100x, you have doubled the value of your entire portfolio."

I was really starting to understand the psychology of this approach. The essence is never to risk more than you can afford to lose emotionally and financially, and always to maintain a controlled degree of exposure to unlimited upside potential. You can sleep soundly knowing your foundation is secure while still participating in the revolutionary wealth-creation potential of crypto.

The Real-Time Risk Decision

As if summoned by our discussion, Charlie's phone buzzed with a market alert. Bitcoin had just dropped by 12% on news of regulatory uncertainty caused by a major government announcement. The notification lit all our phones up simultaneously, prompting Simon's face to tighten with remembered trauma.

"Perfect timing," Charlie said, looking at Simon. "Let's walk through a real-time risk decision using the framework we just discussed. This is your chance to learn to think how professionals think, compared with how your traumatized brain wants you to react."

We could see a series of charts on Charlie's main monitor. Each red candle resembled a wound from a knife, as the lifeblood seeped from Bitcoin's price before our eyes.

"Tell me what your mind is telling you to do right now," Charlie asked Simon.

Simon's response came quickly, his voice tight with anxiety. "Bitcoin is crashing. It's probably going lower. This could be the start of a bear market. Maybe I should sell everything and wait for the bottom. Or maybe... maybe this is when I should use leverage to buy the dip and make back what I lost?"

"Perfect," Charlie said. "You just demonstrated both forms of amateur thinking, panic selling and revenge trading. Now let's walk through how a professional would analyze this exact situation."

Charlie opened a document titled 'Regulatory FUD Response Protocol' and began to walk us through it systematically.

Step One: Threat Assessment

Q1: Does this news fundamentally change the long-term Bitcoin investment thesis?

Q2: Are there specific regulatory actions or is this just political posturing?

Q3: How have similar regulatory concerns been resolved historically?

As we pondered the answers to these items on the questionnaire, Charlie pulled up historical data showing dozens of similar regulatory scares over the years. Each had caused sharp drops. Each had soon been followed by recovery and new highs.

Step Two: Opportunity Evaluation

Q1: Are the current prices creating attractive risk-reward ratios?

Q2: Is market-wide fear creating temporary mispricing relative to the fundamentals?

Q3: Do we have capital available to deploy systematically?

Alongside these questions, Charlie showed valuation models suggesting that at that moment, Bitcoin was 20% below fair value based on network metrics and adoption curves.

Step Three: Risk Management

Q1: What's the maximum additional downside if these regulatory concerns worsen?

Q2: How does this affect overall portfolio risk?

Q3: Are we positioned to survive the various scenarios?

The analysis demonstrated that even in the worst-case scenarios, Bitcoin dropping by another 30–40% would not threaten the survival of a properly constructed portfolio.

Step Four: Systematic Response

Task 1: Execute the predetermined plan for regulatory uncertainty scenarios.

Task 2: Maintain discipline regardless of emotional reactions.

Task 3: Focus on long-term positioning rather than short-term predictions.

Charlie pulled up his own trading account and showed us his responses to these guidelines. We saw modest additional buying through predetermined limit orders that represented about 5% of his cash reserves and was spread across multiple price levels.

"Notice," Charlie advised Simon, "that professional risk analysis doesn't try to predict what will happen. Instead, it asks how to position optimally given that multiple scenarios are possible. I can't know whether Bitcoin will drop another 20% or rocket back up by 30%. But I do know that systematic accumulation during periods of fear has been the single best strategy for building long-term wealth in this space."

Simon watched the process intently. "So, you're not trying to time the bottom?"

"Timing the bottom is gambling," Charlie replied. "Systematic accumulation during fear is investing. One requires prediction. The other only requires discipline."

Advanced Risk Psychology

As our marathon session stretched toward dawn, Charlie revealed one final framework: the advanced psychological techniques used by the most successful institutional investors.

"At the highest levels," he explained, "risk management becomes less about mathematical calculations and more about psychologically preparing for uncertainty. The math is simple. It's the psychology that's complex."

Mental Rehearsal

"Every week, spend time visualizing different portfolio scenarios, including significant losses. Envisage yourself responding calmly and systematically. Practice your emotional responses to various crisis situations. If you have mentally rehearsed a 50% drawdown 20 times, when it actually happens, your brain recognizes it as a familiar rather than threatening event."

Outcome Independence

"Develop satisfaction based on good decision-making regardless of the outcome. A good decision that loses money is still a good decision.

A bad decision that makes money is still a bad decision. When you truly internalize this concept, you become psychologically bulletproof."

The Antifragile Mindset

"View crises as opportunities rather than threats. Develop excitement about market dislocations and the buying opportunities they represent. Build systems that will benefit from volatility rather than struggle because of it. And always maintain optimism about the long-term outcomes while preparing for short-term challenges."

"The ultimate goal," Charlie concluded as the first rays of sunlight began to stream through his study windows, "is to develop psychological antifragility. You want to become an investor who gets stronger and more capable with each crisis rather than weaker. Someone who sees market crashes as gifts rather than catastrophes. Someone with such robust risk management behaviors that volatility becomes your friend rather than your enemy."

Simon stood to leave, looking exhausted but transformed. "Six months ago, I thought my investing career was over. Now I realize it's just beginning, but this time it will be built on a foundation that can't be destroyed."

The Recovery Success Story

Six months later, Simon called me out of the blue with an update that perfectly illustrated the power of systematic risk management. His voice was worlds away from that traumatic call in the dead of the night. It was calm, confident, even excited.

"I wanted to thank you," he said. "Not just for supporting my financial recovery, though that's been incredible. But for teaching me how to think about risk properly. It's changed everything."

Simon's recovery had exceeded all expectations. By following the framework religiously, he had rebuilt 60% of his lost capital through systematic investing. But more importantly, he had redesigned his psychological relationship with risk.

"The most incredible part," Simon continued, "is that I'm actually making better investment decisions now than before I lost everything. The trauma has forced me to develop real discipline toward risk management. I sleep better now holding crypto positions than I ever did before, even though the market is just as volatile."

Simon shared his new approach: "Every Sunday, I take the time to review my portfolio using Charlie's institutional framework. I ask myself: Is anything threatening my survival? No, because I keep six months' worth of expenses in cash and never use leverage. Am I positioned for opportunities? Yes, because I keep 20% in dry powder for market dislocations. Am I taking intelligent risks? Yes, because I have small positions in15 different emerging protocols, any of which could go to zero without affecting my psychology or lifestyle."

"But here's what really changed," Simon said, the slight smile seemingly audible. "I used to check prices every hour, my mood swinging with every movement. Now I check them maybe once a week. I know my risk is managed, my position sizing is appropriate, and time is on my side. The market's volatility has become irrelevant to my emotional state."

Simon had discovered what many professional investors eventually learn: proper risk management doesn't limit returns; it enables them by allowing you to stay invested through multiple market cycles, capturing the exponential growth that comes from increasing adoption and scarcity.

Chapter 5 Key Takeaways

Risk Mastery protects and builds wealth through psychological preparation:

1. **Eliminate survival risk** – Never risk money you need for living or continued investing. Your ability to stay in the game matters more than any single opportunity.

2. **Think in risk hierarchies** – After eliminating survival risk, opportunity risk must be managed, and only then can you consider taking optimization risks for enhanced returns.

3. **Build antifragile portfolios** – Use barbell strategies with 80% in stable assets and 20% in asymmetric opportunities. Avoid the deadly middle ground.

4. **Practice psychological preparation** – Mental rehearsal and scenario planning prevent emotional decisions. Train your mind like an athlete trains their body.

5. **Focus on process over outcomes** – Good risk management enables long-term wealth building. Develop satisfaction from making good decisions regardless of the short-term results.

Your Homework

Complete the following risk assessment and management exercises:

- **Risk Audit**: List every position in your portfolio. Identify any Level 1 (survival) risks. These must be eliminated immediately, regardless of the potential opportunity cost.

- **Scenario Planning**: Write out your specific response plan for

- these scenarios: 50% market crash, regulatory ban, largest position going to zero. Your plans should be systematic, not emotional.

- **Position Sizing Review**: Ensure no single crypto position (except Bitcoin / Ethereum) exceeds 5% of your portfolio. Speculative positions should occupy 1–2% maximum.

- **Mental Rehearsal**: Spend 10 minutes visualizing a major market crash. See yourself responding calmly, checking your written plan, and executing systematically. Practice until the scenario feels familiar rather than threatening.

- **Create Your Risk Framework**: Write down your personal risk management rules. Post them where you will see them during market volatility. These rules will save you when emotions run high.

Next Lesson: The Discipline Engine

How to build automatic systems that make good decisions when willpower fails.

Charlie reveals the mechanical frameworks that prevent emotional mistakes and create consistent wealth-building behaviors, even under maximum psychological pressure. You will learn why discipline is not about strength but about systems, and how to build an investment process that works especially when you don't.

"Professional investors don't ask 'What could I gain?' They ask, 'What could I lose, and how do I protect against it?' This single shift in perspective separates wealth builders from wealth destroyers."

- Charlie's Third Law of Professional Risk Management

CHAPTER 6

THE DISCIPLINE ENGINE

*How to Build Automatic Systems That Make Good
Decisions When Willpower Alone Fails*

The Analyst Who Forgot Her Training

The email arrived at 6:30AM on a Monday, marked urgent in red.

From: Alice Wu <a.wu@alphaedge.com>

Subject: URGENT - Charlie said you'd understand

Casey,

You don't know me, but Charlie gave me your contact after I attended his workshop last month. Said you'd rebuilt your entire approach after a crisis.

Three weeks ago, I had everything figured out. Perfect system. Systematic approach. 18 months of pristine execution.

Today I'm staring at 43 trades I made in a single night. My own portfolio. The one I show other PMs as a model.

I teach behavioral finance. I WROTE our firm's discipline protocols.

But when my mother's diagnosis came the same week David left, something broke. I watched myself destroy everything I'd built, fully aware it was wrong, completely unable to stop.

Charlie said you knew someone who builds systems for when discipline fails. Because knowing what to do clearly isn't enough.

Can we talk?

- Alice

P.S. I know how this looks. Hedge fund analyst asking a retail investor for help. But I'm desperate.

I read it twice, remembering my own 3AM crisis. The difference was striking, I panicked from inexperience. Alice had fallen despite her expertise.

I called immediately.

"Thank you for coming back to me," she said, exhaustion coating every word. "I need you to understand one thing. I've been managing institutional money for seven years. Never once broke protocol. Until three weeks ago."

Her story unfolded with surgical precision, the analyst in her documenting her own downfall.

"Thursday, was the fourth night at the hospital. Mom asked about treatment costs that weren't covered by insurance. I just wanted to check my portfolio value. One quick look."

She laughed bitterly. "One look became recalculating positions. Then 'protecting gains.' Then revenge trading to fix my mistakes. By dawn, I'd executed 43 trades. My annual average is 48."

The silence stretched between us.

"I know every cognitive bias that attacked me," Alice continued. "I can name them: emotional hijacking from grief, decision fatigue from the hospital, loss aversion from needing liquidity. I teach this. But knowledge wasn't enough."

I knew exactly whom she needed to meet.

The Man Who Automated Discipline

Dr. Byron Webb operated out of an unassuming office in a medical building downtown, but his reputation in behavioral psychology was legendary. While other researchers merely studied why people fail under pressure, Byron focused on something far more useful: how to build psychological systems that continued to function even when human judgment broke down.

His office told the story. No motivational posters or inspiring quotes here. Instead, every surface demonstrated systematic design. The coffeemaker started automatically at 5:45AM. The lights adjusted themselves in response to time and the weather. His desktop could only access research papers until noon, email between noon and 2PM, and then locked everything except his writing software after 2PM.

"I studied discipline," Byron explained as Alice and I settled into chairs that had been precisely arranged for our visit, "because I had none. Lost my kids' college funds day-trading tech stocks in 1999. Destroyed my marriage trying to win it back in 2000. The pain of watching my wife pack our children's belongings was immense, knowing I had gambled away their future. It was this that drove 20 subsequent years of research into systematic behavior."

He started to open files containing brain scans as he spoke. "Discipline is the most misunderstood concept in human performance. Most people think discipline is about willpower, that is, the ability to force yourself to do things you don't want to do. They imagine it like a muscle you can strengthen."

Byron shook his head with the conviction of someone who had learned through painful experience. "But that's exactly wrong. Research shows that truly disciplined people use less willpower, not more. They have built automatic systems that make good decisions without requiring continuous conscious effort or emotional control."

The brain scans were remarkable. During challenging tasks, disciplined individuals showed decreased activity in regions associated with self-control and increased activity in areas associated with automatic processing. Their brains were not fighting harder, in fact they weren't fighting at all.

"Think of willpower like the battery in your phone," Byron continued. "Every decision drains it. Every stressful moment depletes it faster. Every emotional challenge is like running a power-hungry app. Most people try to get a bigger battery. The effort just exhausts them further. But what if you could run your investments on a completely different power source?"

Alice leaned forward, recognizing herself in the metaphor. "My battery was completely dead. Three weeks of hospital visits, the break-up, work stress — I had nothing left."

"Exactly," Byron said. "And that's when you needed discipline most. But you were trying to rely on a dead battery. What you need is a system that runs on household current that's always on, always reliable, independent of how depleted you feel personally."

When Willpower Becomes Your Enemy

Byron walked us through what he called "the willpower paradox", meaning that the harder you try to maintain discipline through force of will, the more likely you are to fail catastrophically.

"Willpower fails in predictable stages," he explained, "like a dam giving way. First comes ego depletion, whereby stress creates hairline cracks in your self-control."

He showed us data from thousands of investment decisions and how they correlated with stress levels. The pattern was unmistakable: as stress increased, decision quality degraded exponentially, not linearly.

"Alice, tell me about the 24 hours before your trading disaster," Byron prompted.

Alice's eyes grew distant. "Mom's oncologist had just recommended an experimental treatment. Except that her insurance would not cover it and I'd be $200,000 out of pocket. I had not slept for three days. My ex-fiancé had texted asking about dividing our assets. It felt like my entire life was spinning out of control."

"And your portfolio was the one thing you could control," Byron said gently. "Or so your depleted brain told you."

He pulled up a slide showing the neurological cascade of failing willpower. "When ego depletion reaches critical levels, your prefrontal cortex (the rational decision-maker) literally goes offline. Blood flow decreases. Electrical activity drops. You are trying to make complex financial decisions while suffering the cognitive equivalent of a concussion."

"But here's where it gets insidious," Byron continued. "Your brain doesn't tell you it's impaired. Instead, it creates elaborate justifications for terrible decisions. Tired brains are masterful lawyers, crafting watertight justifications for destructive choices."

Alice nodded painfully. "I remember thinking that my analysis was brilliant that night. 'The market's being irrational,' I told myself. 'I'm the only one seeing clearly.' Every trade felt completely valid in the moment."

"This is the rationalization stage," Byron explained. "It's where discipline truly dies. Not in the moment of weakness, but in the justification that follows. Your brain reframes the destructive behavior as strategic adaptation."

He showed us transcripts taken from traders' commentary during major losses. Their rationalizations were eerily similar: special circumstances, temporary adjustments, protecting capital, seizing opportunities.

All sophisticated-sounding explanations for emotional panic and loss of control.

"Then comes the cascade," Byron said, his voice carrying the weight of personal experience. "One violation becomes permission for 10 more. The first trade breaks the dam. The second widens the crack. By the third, the entire system collapses."

Alice's voice was barely audible. "I went from checking prices to adjusting stops to full-blown leverage trading within hours. Each decision felt connected to the last, like I was solving a problem, but I was really just digging deeper."

Byron pulled up a final chart, recovery time versus cascade duration. "Here's the cruelest part. We know that three weeks of willpower failure typically requires three to six months of systematic rebuilding. The psychological scar tissue makes future discipline even harder. Unless..."

He paused, letting the weight of failed systems sink in.

"...Unless you stop relying on willpower entirely."

Building Your Financial Exoskeleton

"The solution," Byron explained, pulling out highly structured mind maps, isn't to develop stronger willpower. It's to build what I call a 'financial exoskeleton.' These are external systems that maintain perfect discipline irrespective of your internal state."

He spread the diagrams across his desk. They detailed systematic behaviors with the precision of engineering schematics.

"Think of Iron Man," Byron said with a rare smile. "Tony Stark isn't physically strong. The suit is strong. To make up for his limitations, he builds technology that grants him superhuman capabilities.

We are going to build you a suit of systematic behavior that makes superhuman investment discipline automatic."

Byron's schemas revealed four interconnected layers, each designed to function independently while reinforcing the others.

"Layer one is environmental design," Byron explained, tracing the foundation. "At this stage you need to reshape your physical and digital environment to make good decisions automatic and bad decisions impossible."

He showed us the testimonials of his most successful clients. One hedge fund manager said they'd removed every internet-connected device from their home, except for a single laptop that could only access pre-approved financial sites between 9AM and 10AM. Another had hired an assistant whose sole job was to change all trading passwords every Friday and only reinstate them for use on Monday morning.

"Layer two involves installing trigger systems: predetermined responses to specific conditions that execute without your involvement. Think of them as investment reflexes that bypass conscious thought entirely."

Alice studied the schema intently. "So, instead of deciding whether to rebalance, the system decides for me?"

"The system doesn't decide anything," Byron corrected. "You have already decided. The system just executes your pre-programmed decisions when the conditions are met. You become the architect, not the builder."

Layer three contained details of decision protocols: written rules covering every conceivable scenario, from 10% market corrections to 50% crashes, and from sudden wealth to financial emergency.

Each protocol included specific actions, mandatory waiting periods, and accountability checkpoints.

"Layer four is the feedback mechanism," Byron continued. "The system monitors itself, tracks compliance, and evolves based on results. It learns and improves without requiring your conscious attention."

Alice looked skeptical. "This sounds like it would take enormous effort and expense to maintain."

Byron shook his head. "That's the beautiful paradox. Yes, building the system does require intense initial effort. But once built, it requires zero willpower to maintain. It's the difference between pushing a car and driving one. Same destination, completely different effort."

The Portfolio Manager Who Never Has to Decide

To illustrate the power of systematic discipline, Byron shared the story of James Sterling, a portfolio manager who had built a $200 million fund using purely automated decision-making.

"James came to me in 2009," Byron began, pulling up a photo of an exhausted-looking man in an expensive suit. "Brilliant analyst with a perfect track record through 2007. He had predicted the housing crisis, positioned his fund to profit from it. His analysis was flawless."

Byron showed us James's pre-crisis research. Page after page of meticulous scrutiny predicting exactly what would happen to mortgage-backed securities, bank stocks, and credit markets. It read like a prophecy of the financial apocalypse.

"But when the crisis actually hit," Byron continued, "something unexpected happened. James found himself unable to execute his own plan. He would watch CNBC all day, paralyzed."

He had written detailed instructions for profiting from the crisis yet couldn't pull the trigger on his own trades."

As the photos progressed, James's physical deterioration through 2008 became all too clear. He gained 40 pounds. Developed a tremor. Started drinking to calm his nerves enough to trade.

"By December 2008, at the absolute bottom, James panicked. Sold everything. That locked in massive losses for his clients. His perfect analysis became worthless because he couldn't act on it. The very next quarter, exactly as his research had predicted, markets began their recovery. The trades he had abandoned would have returned 400%."

Alice winced. "That's almost worse than being wrong. Knowing you were right but being unable to act on it."

"James thought so too," Byron said grimly. "That's when he came to me. Suicidal ideation. Destroyed reputation. But he was also possessed of absolute clarity: while his analytical mind was brilliant, his execution was fatally flawed."

Byron pulled up James's current fund performance, showing a steady upward line with minimal drawdowns over 15 years.

"Today, James manages $2.4 billion in assets. Since we started to work together, his returns have averaged 23% annually with maximum drawdowns of 8%. Want to know his secret?"

We leaned in.

"James never makes investment decisions anymore. Ever."

Byron let that sink in before explaining. "Every position in his fund is determined by mathematical formulas he developed in a cold state during calmer market periods. Entry points are triggered automatically based on predetermined criteria.

Position sizes calculate themselves. Rebalancing happens on schedule. He's not allowed to override anything."

"But surely he must adjust for new information?" Alice asked.

"He adjusts the formulas on a quarterly basis, during scheduled reviews with a management committee. But he cannot touch live trades. Think of him as the architect who designs buildings but isn't allowed on construction sites."

Byron showed us James's daily routine. After arriving at his office at 8AM, he reviewed system performance, researched new strategies, and refined future formulas. But a software lock prevented him from accessing the trading systems. Even his own fund was off-limits except during the quarterly formula updates.

"The results speak for themselves," Byron noted. "His worst year's performance since implementing the system was +11%. His best was +47%. More importantly, he sleeps eight hours a night and hasn't had a drink in 12 years."

"Because he doesn't carry the stress of decision-making," I observed.

"Exactly. His brain does what it does best, which is analysis and strategy. The system does what it does best, which is consistent execution. They only really need to interact once a quarter."

Engineering Your Investment Environment

Byron handed Alice a leather-bound workbook titled "The Discipline Engine: Construction Manual." It felt substantial, serious.

"Building systematic discipline starts with environmental engineering," he explained. "Most people try to resist temptation. We are going to go one better. We'll eliminate it entirely."

He walked us through the first phase like a contractor explaining a renovation. "Week one is demolition. You are going to remove every pathway to impulsive decisions."

Alice opened the workbook to find specific, actionable steps:

"First, your phone," Byron said, pulling out his own device. "This is my biggest trigger, so I have engineered it to completely avoid temptation." His phone had no browser, no app store access, no financial apps whatsoever. "It's a communication device, nothing more."

"But how do you…?" Alice began.

"I have a separate tablet for financial review," Byron explained. "Locked in my office. It's only accessible during predetermined hours. The physical separation creates the psychological separation I need."

Leafing through the workbook revealed dozens of detailed environmental modifications for every situation. There were password managers that changed trading passwords automatically, browser extensions that blocked access to financial platforms except during specific hours, or physical timers that locked devices in charging safes.

"I had one client," Byron recalled, "a day trader who was trying to become a long-term investor. We literally removed the internet from his house so that he had to drive to a coffee shop to check positions. The friction eliminated 95% of his impulse trading."

Alice looked overwhelmed. "This seems slightly extreme."

"Extreme problems require extreme solutions," Byron replied. "You lost two years of gains in three weeks. How extreme can it get?"

He was right. Alice nodded slowly and began working through the environmental checklist, face shifting from skepticism to determination.

"The beautiful thing about environmental design," Byron noted, "is that it works as soon as your system's in place. You don't need to develop new habits or strengthen willpower. You simply make bad decisions an impossibility."

Beyond Human Discipline

We re-convened after three months, and during that session, Byron revealed the advanced systematic approaches that the most sophisticated institutional investors used, systems that transcended human discipline entirely.

"At the highest levels," he explained, showing us examples of proprietary trading algorithms, "investment discipline becomes pure technology. Humans design systems, but humans don't run them."

He showed us lines of code that looked more like space mission protocols than investment strategies, explaining that companies like Renaissance Technologies had an approach that removed human judgment from daily operations entirely. Algorithms analyzed millions of datapoints, calculated position sizes to 12 decimal places, and executed trades in microseconds. Humans could suggest strategy modifications during quarterly reviews but couldn't touch live trading.

"This isn't about replacing human intelligence," Byron clarified. "It's about deploying human intelligence optimally. The analysts' brilliant minds design strategies during calm, rational periods. Technology then executes those strategies during chaotic periods, removing the potential for human emotional responses to sabotage effective systems."

He showed us what traders' brain scans looked like when using fully systematic approaches versus discretionary trading. The systematic traders' stress regions remained all-but dormant, even during major market dislocations. They watched their systems work like engineers monitoring automated factories.

"The paradox," Byron noted, "is that removing human control enhances human performance. When you aren't worried about execution, you can focus entirely on strategy. When you aren't stressed about individual trades, you can think in terms of decades instead of days."

Alice had been taking notes throughout, but now she looked up with renewed understanding. "It's so true. The goal isn't to become more disciplined. It's to make discipline irrelevant."

"Exactly," Byron agreed. "A fish doesn't need discipline to swim. It's built for water. You are building for yourselves an investment environment where good decisions happen as naturally as breathing."

He pulled out one final framework, a comprehensive schema for total systematic investing:

The Five Pillars of Systematic Discipline:

First Pillar: Environmental Architecture. Every aspect of the investor's environment is designed to make good decisions automatic and bad decisions impossible. Physical spaces, digital tools, and social structures must all align with the chosen systematic principles.

Second Pillar: Decision Protocols. Written procedures for every conceivable scenario, developed during calm periods and executed automatically without deviation during times of stress. Like a pilot's emergency checklist, no thinking is required, just systematic execution.

Third Pillar: Execution Automation. Technology that implements decisions seamlessly, removing human intervention from the process. From simple dollar-cost averaging to complex algorithmic rebalancing, machines execute human strategy.

Fourth Pillar: Feedback Loops. Systems that monitor their own performance, track compliance, and evolve based on the results. Not requiring human attention but benefiting from human analysis during scheduled reviews.

Fifth Pillar: Continuous Evolution. Regular optimization of systems based on new knowledge and changing conditions. Changes are implemented systematically, not impulsively, with mandatory testing periods and gradual roll-outs.

"The ultimate goal," Byron concluded as our session ended, "is to build an investment system that functions like a well-designed building. It stands regardless of weather, requires minimal maintenance, and serves its purpose without daily human intervention. You become the architect, not the construction worker."

Alice stood to leave, workbook clutched like a lifeline. But her posture had changed. Three months ago, she had arrived broken by the failure of her own expertise. Now she radiated quiet confidence, not in her discipline, but in her systems.

"One last thing," Byron added. "People will tell you this approach is too rigid, too mechanical. That it removes the 'art' from investing. When they do, ask them about their returns during their last personal crisis. Then show them yours."

The Metamorphosis

Another six months later, Alice called with an update. It was a huge relief that she sounded like a different person entirely.

"I need to tell you what happened last week," she began, excitement rippling through her voice. "My ex reached out on Tuesday, wanting to 'talk about us.'

Normally, that would send me into an emotional tailspin. Check crypto obsessively, make stupid trades trying to feel in control."

"What happened next?" I asked.

"Nothing happened. That's the miracle. I couldn't check the prices all week because my phone doesn't have that capability anymore. Even better, my laptop was locked in my time-delay safe until Saturday morning. By the time I could access my portfolio, the emotional storm had passed."

She laughed, a sound I had not heard from her for some months. "The system protected me from myself. My portfolio kept executing its systematic plan while I dealt with life events. When I finally checked on Saturday, I was up 3% for the week."

Alice talked us through the complete transformation statistics, but it was clear that the numbers told only part of the story. "I sleep much better now," Alice continued. "Eight hours straight. No midnight price checking because it's literally impossible. No decision fatigue because I don't make the small decisions. The system makes them for me."

"But here's the most incredible part," she added. "I'm definitely a better analyst now. Without the stress of execution, my mind is free to research, strategize, and think long-term. It's freed me up to develop new systematic strategies that I will implement next quarter."

She paused, clearly relishing the next thought before she was ready to share the deepest change. "My mom asked me last week if I was worried about paying for her treatment. For the first time in my life, I could honestly say that I wasn't. Not because I have enough money, but because I have a system that will preserve and grow what money I do have regardless of what life throws at me."

The contrast with her panic-driven calls nine months earlier was profound. She had transformed from a brilliant analyst whose execution became flawed in a crisis to a systematic investor who was now immune to emotional interference.

"Dr. Webb was right," Alice concluded. "I don't have more discipline now. I have better systems. The discipline is built into the enviroment, not relying on my willpower."

Chapter 6 Key Takeaways

The Discipline Engine automates good decisions and eliminates failure of willpower:

1. **Willpower is unreliable** – Stress, fatigue, and emotion all deplete the mental resources needed for self-discipline. Relying on willpower for important decisions is like relying on a dying battery.

2. **Build automatic systems** – Create mechanical processes that make good decisions regardless of your psychological state. Become the architect of systems, not the executor of individual trades.

3. **Engineer your environment** – Remove temptations and friction for bad decisions, create the conditions that support good ones. Make impulsive trading physically impossible.

4. **Use technology systematically** – Modern tools can create discipline systems that are impossible to maintain manually. Let machines handle execution while humans handle strategy.

5. **Monitor and optimize continuously** – Track system adherence and refine processes based on results. Evolve systematically, not impulsively.

Your Homework

Build your personal discipline engine, starting today:

- **Environmental Audit**: List every device, app, and website you use for investing. Identify which enables impulsive decisions. Begin the removal process immediately.

- **Technology Separation**: Set up a dedicated device for financial review. Remove all financial capabilities from the devices you use every day. Create physical separation between you and your portfolio.

- **Decision Protocols**: Write specific procedures for three scenarios: 20% market drop, 30% portfolio gain, and personal crisis. Include exact steps, no judgment calls allowed.

- **Automation Set-up**: Implement at least one automatic system this week, be it dollar-cost averaging, rebalancing alerts, or password rotation. Start simple, expand gradually.

- **Accountability Structure**: Share your systematic rules with someone you trust. Give them permission to enforce your rules when you are tempted to break them.

Next Lesson: The Compound Advantage

How small psychological improvements create exponential wealth differences over time.

Charlie reveals why tiny behavioral changes compound into massive wealth differences, and how to identify the highest-leverage improvements to your investment psychology. You will discover why making just 1% better decisions creates 100% better outcomes over decades.

"Truly disciplined people actually use less willpower, not more. They have built automatic systems that make good decisions without requiring conscious effort or emotional control."

- Dr. Byron Webb's First Law of Systematic Discipline

CHAPTER 7

THE EXPONENTIAL EDGE

*How Small Psychological Improvements Create
Exponential Wealth Differences Over Time*

The Invitation That Changed Everything

I almost threw the letter away. Another investment conference spam, I thought, until I saw my name handwritten in Charlie's distinctive script above the typed address. My hands trembled slightly as I read the invitation, not from excitement, but out of a peculiar mix of confusion and dread.

"The Global Institute for Behavioral Finance (GIBF) cordially invites you to present your findings on psychological arbitrage at our upcoming Annual Summit. Your work with Dr Charlie Alexander, a Senior Member of this Institute, has demonstrated the potential for measurable, non-linear improvements in long-term investment returns. We consider this worthy of further academic study. Your research may help explain why small psychological improvements create exponential wealth differences over time.

Full details of the upcoming Summit, along with joining instructions are enclosed.

We look forward to hearing from you and hope that you will agree to participate in our prestigious event"

Present? Research? There was no way I considered myself a researcher. I was just someone trying to keep my finger off the sell button during crashes and the buy button during pumps.

When I called Charlie, his reaction was immediate and enthusiastic, in stark contrast to my rising panic.

"Congratulations," he said before I could even explain why I was calling. "The GIBF only invites people whose research has uncovered behavioral changes that could create measurable statistical differences in investment outcomes."

"But I haven't done any research! My work isn't…"

"Haven't you?" Charlie interrupted. I could hear him tapping on his keyboard as he spoke. "Ever since that night two years ago, you've tracked every investment decision, every emotional response, every systematic improvement. That's 24 months of data, one of the most comprehensive datasets on monitoring investment psychology that I have ever seen."

He rattled off statistics I had forgotten I'd been collecting. "In that time, your returns have improved by 23% annually since implementing stronger psychological frameworks. Your maximum drawdowns have decreased by 67%. And your adherence to systematic investing protocols has increased from 34% to 94%."

My mouth went dry. Eventually, I found words to describe my horror: "Charlie, I can't present at an academic conference. I will embarrass myself. I'll embarrass you."

"The only thing that would embarrass me," Charlie said firmly, "is if you let imposter syndrome prevent you from sharing insights that could transform the lives of thousands of other investors."

Entering the Cathedral of Compound Wealth

The summit was held at a private research institute that felt more like a modern monastery than an academic building. Glass and steel twisted skyward inside impossible spires, designed to make you look up, think big, consider the infinite.

Inside, the walls displayed wealth accumulation charts in which seemingly fantastical curves reached exponentially toward numbers that made my middle-class brain short-circuit. But what struck me most were my fellow attendees. These were not the loud, aggressive traders

I had encountered at crypto conferences in the past. They moved with an unhurried confidence, spoke in measured tones, and had the relaxed bearing of people who had figured something out that the rest of us were still searching for.

In the lobby, Dr. Grace Tan, the conference director, greeted me personally. She possessed the kind of dignified presence that compelled you to stand straighter without realizing it.

"We have been following your work with Charlie with great interest," she said as we walked toward the main conference hall. "Your psychological transformation represents exactly the kind of behavioral change we study. These small improvements you've made compound into extraordinary differences over time."

Glancing sideways at her calm profile, I felt like a community college student who had accidentally wandered into Harvard. "I think there might be some mistake. I'm not an academic"

"Neither are most of our presenters," Dr. Tan smiled. "We study practitioners, not theorists. Your real-world transformation is worth more than a dozen theoretical papers."

The conference hall delivered me a huge spike of cortisol. Three hundred seats were arranged in amphitheater style, all focused on a central stage. My presentation was scheduled for 3PM. That gave me five hours in which to either prepare or panic.

I chose panic.

The Two-Million Dollar Difference

Dr. Tan opened the summit with a presentation that prompted the entire room to lean forward as one.

"Welcome to the study of compound advantage," she announced.

"Today we are examining how and why small improvements in ivestment psychology can create exponential differences in long-term wealth outcomes."

The first slide appeared, drawing actual gasps from the audience. These were numbers of such magnitude, even the hardened fund managers and academics in the room were visibly shocked.

She clicked through a range of wealth accumulation patterns, depending on the behavioral characteristics of different investors. The curves started close together but diverged dramatically over time, the way that rockets on even slightly different trajectories would end up on different planets.

"The average retail investor turns $100,000 into $230,000 over 20 years," Dr. Tan explained. "Whereas the psychologically optimized investor turns the same capital into $2.8 million in that time. Same markets. Same opportunities. The only difference is psychology."

I did some quick mental math. My initial crypto investment of $50,000, if I maintained psychological optimization, could become... I stopped calculating. The number seemed impossible.

A fund manager in the row ahead of me whispered to his colleague, "If this is even half true, we need to restructure our entire training program."

Fortified by the weight of years of research, Dr Tan continued: "As you can see, the difference between average and optimized investor psychology is worth over $2.5 million on a $100,000 initial investment. And this difference compounds exponentially over time."

She paused, letting the implications sink in. "Small behavioral iprovements don't create small differences.

They create exponential, generational wealth gaps for individuals and firms willing to master them. The question is: which trajectory are you on?"

When Math Meets Mind

Professor Julian Vane, a quantitative psychologist from MIT, took the stage with the energy of someone about to reveal the location of buried treasure. And in a way, he was.

Without even a preliminary greeting, he launched straight in: "We have analyzed the investment returns of over 10,000 individuals" Vane announced. "If you simply reduce your 'emotional' trades, meaning trades that deviate from your pre-set plan by 80%, you add an average of 2.3% to your annual return."

He paused for effect. "That sounds small. But compound an extra 2.3% over 20 years, and you end up with 57% more total wealth than the person who 'followed their gut.' That is the power of a single behavioral change."

The results are so consistent they have forced us to reconsider everything we thought we knew about market returns."

As he went through his presentation, the data behind him made me pull out my notebook and start calculating my own improvements.

I scribbled frantically. Since starting to work with Charlie my emotion-led trading had dropped from 73% of decisions to 12%. That meant...

"But here's where it gets interesting," he continued, seemingly oblivious to the rising anticipation in the room. "These improvements stack multiplicatively, not additively. Master all three primary psychological factors, and you do not get an 11% improvement.

The compound interaction creates returns that could transform entire family trajectories."

At that moment, every eye in the room was focused on what he called the High-Leverage Improvement Hierarchy:

Foundation Skills — These Create 80% of Your Advantage:

- Emotional Regulation Under Stress: +3.5% annually

- Long-Term Perspective Maintenance: +2.8% annually

- Systematic Discipline Implementation: +2.1% annually

"Focus here first," Professor Vane advised, his laser pointer circling the three items. "These foundational skills are simple to understand but challenging to master. Do that, and they can create exponential wealth differences. Emotional regulation alone has the potential to add 3.5% to your annual returns. Compound that over 20 years and that single skill could effectively double your wealth."

He paused, scanning the room. "Most investors chase complex strategies while ignoring the basics. It is like trying to run a marathon without learning to walk. Master these three factors, and you will already have separated yourself from 90% of investors."

I found myself quickly revisiting my calculations. If I improved all three, that was... over 7% additional annual return... just from improving my mindset. No market timing needed. Just emotional control, long-term thinking, and systematic behavior.

"The tragedy," he concluded, "is that these skills are entirely learnable. Anyone can develop them. But most people never will, because they are looking for market secrets instead of psychological solutions."

A woman behind me whispered to the person beside her, "I have been managing money for 20 years and never understood why some clients dramatically outperformed. This explains everything."

Jasmin and Michael: A Tale of Two Futures

Dr. Tan returned to the stage with what she called "the most important case study in behavioral finance." But instead of showing another slide deck, she did something unexpected.

"Jasmin and Michael, would you please join me on stage?"

Two people rose from the audience. Both appeared to be in their mid-40s, professionally dressed, clearly successful. But something was different between them. Jasmin moved with a calm assurance while Michael seemed to carry an invisible weight.

Once they were seated on the stage, both turned their heads to face Dr Tan. "Fifteen years ago," she explained, "these two people began investing. Their circumstances were identical. Same age, same income, same initial capital. Jasmin received psychological training using the principles outlined by Professor Vane. Michael, however, followed conventional wisdom. Today, they have agreed to share their stories."

Jasmin spoke first, her voice steady. "In 2008, I watched my portfolio drop by 40%. Even in the depths of the financial crisis, my training kicked in, not my emotions. I had a protocol for market crashes, developed when I was calm. I followed my protocol mechanically. I increased my monthly investments and rebalanced, which meant my system forced me to buy more of the assets everyone else was dumping. It felt insane to put money into a falling market, but I trusted the system over my own survival instincts.

Michael's story was daunting by comparison. "I thought I was being smart in 2008. Sold everything to 'protect' my capital then waited for the 'right time' to get back in. That time never felt right so I ended up missing the entire recovery. Made the same mistake in 2020. And again, with crypto in 2022." As the members of the audience shifted awkwardly, you could see his words had ignited some painful memories.

Dr. Tan displayed their results. The disparity was shocking, even though I had seen the earlier presentation:

Jasmin's portfolio: $2.1 million

Michael's portfolio: $740,000

"Same income," Dr. Tan emphasized. "Same markets. Same opportunities. The difference was systematic psychological training versus emotional decision-making."

Michael's voice cracked slightly. "The hardest part isn't the money; we're comfortable enough. It's the realization of the 'Behavioral Tax' I paid. Jasmin's kids have a structural advantage, a level of wealth that functions like an engine, compounding on its own. Mine have a safety net. Both are good, but only one of us built a system that truly removed the ceiling from their future."

The room was silent. This was not abstract theory anymore. These were real people, real consequences, and real generational legacy.

Jasmin added quietly, "The training wasn't complicated. Just consistent. Small improvements, maintained over time. But those small improvements changed everything."

Inside the Investor's Brain

Next, Dr. Claudie Metzger, brought something quite different to the stage.

She was a neuroscientist who specialized in studying investors brain patterns and it soon became clear we were going to be party to a live brain-scanning demonstration.

"We are going to show you the effect of psychological training on your brain," she announced. "We are extremely lucky to have James with us, a volunteer who has agreed to make investment decisions while we monitor his neural activity in real time. Obviously, this is for educational purposes only and James' own money or any third party's is not at risk as a result of this demonstration."

The volunteer was James, a fund manager who had undergone psychological training five years earlier. As Dr. Metzger showed him scenarios of market crashes, bubbles, and volatility, we watched his brain respond on massive screens.

"Notice the amygdala (the fear center) remains calm even during extreme market scenarios," Dr. Metzger explained. "Now watch what happens when we show the same scenarios to someone without psychological training."

The contrast was stark. The untrained brain lit up in all the wrong places, fear centers blazing while rational regions dimmed and stress hormones flooded the system.

"This is permanent rewiring," Dr. Metzger emphasized. "Psychological training done well doesn't just have the potential to change your behavior, it can fundamentally reconstruct how your brain will process future financial decisions."

I thought about my own transformation. Twenty-one months ago, a 10% drop in the markets would have sent me into a panic spiral. Yet last week, I had watched a crash of 25% while calmly eating breakfast, then executed my predetermined buying protocol without so much as a spike in heart rate.

"The compound advantage," Dr. Metzger concluded, "starts in your neurons. As you can see from our subjects, new pathways are formed over time. Better wiring creates better decisions. Better decisions create better returns. Better returns over time create exponential wealth.

It all begins with training your brain to respond differently to the same stimuli everyone else panics over."

My Turn on the Podium

At 2:47PM, my phone buzzed with a reminder I hardly needed. Thirteen minutes until my presentation. My hands were sweating so badly I could barely grip my notes.

"You will be fine," said a voice behind me. It was Jasmin, the investor from the case study. "The first time I presented here, I had a panic attack the night before. Now I keynote every year. Just share your truth."

At 3:00PM exactly, Dr. Tan introduced me. The walk to the podium felt like a mile. Three hundred pairs of eyes tracked my movement to the center of the stage. Placing my notes on the lectern, I looked up at the sea of fund managers who controlled billions, academics who had written the textbooks I had studied, and successful investors who had mastered what I was still learning.

"Twenty-one months ago," I began, my voice steadying gradually as I spoke, "I was the poster child for every bad investing behavior you have seen today. Emotional trading, no discipline, checking prices every hour, panic selling, FOMO buying. I had all the knowledge but none of the psychology."

I clicked to my first slide, which charted my actual trading history from two years ago. The audience leaned in, recognizing the chaotic pattern of someone who was trading on pure emotion.

"This is what my investment decisions looked like before psychological training. And this," I clicked to the next slide, "is what they look like now."

The transformation was visual poetry. Chaos had become order. Emotion had become system. Reaction had become strategy.

"Let me talk you through the exact changes and their measured impact..."

As I presented my data, something in me shifted. The nervousness melted away, replaced by a growing excitement to share what I had learned. These were not just numbers, they were proof that transformation was possible, that psychology could be trained, that exponential wealth was achievable.

"The most profound change," I found myself saying, departing from my notes, "is that I now make better decisions automatically. Instead of fighting my psychological impulses, I have re-programmed them. The compound advantage isn't about trying harder, it's about becoming someone who doesn't need to try."

The applause was immediate and sustained. But more importantly, I was met by recognition in faces throughout the room, from investors who saw their own potential transformation in my journey.

The Compound Effect in Action

During the break after my presentation, I was unable to even get a cup of coffee, so surrounded was I by institutional investors wanting to discuss implementation. Among the crowd, one conversation stood out.

"My team and I manage $5 billion," said Dr. Kim, her business card reading 'Chief Behavioral Officer', a title I had never seen before. "Your presentation just validated our entire investment approach."

She pulled up data on her tablet showing their fund's performance. "Five years ago, we started requiring all our portfolio managers to undertake psychological training. Look at the results."

The numbers told a story: 4.7% annual outperformance wasn't luck, it was discipline. The 43% reduction in drawdowns meant they lost less when wrong. But the revelation was their 'Protocol Adherence' metric: 89% of the time, their traders followed the plan even when every instinct screamed otherwise. The result? An extra $247 million over five years, purely from better psychology.

"How do you train institutional investors?" I asked.

"Same way you train athletes," she replied. "Systematic practice, continuous measurement, environmental design, and most importantly, removing ego from the equation. Our best performers are the ones who have learned to trust systems over instincts."

Another behavioral economist joined our conversation. He clearly held Dr Kim in high regard. "Our firm is implementing AI coaching systems that detect psychological degradation before it impacts returns. When stress indicators spike, trading permissions automatically become restricted. It's like having a psychological guardian angel."

"The future of investing," Dr. Kim concluded, "isn't finding better opportunities. It's building better brains. The compound advantage belongs to whoever masters psychology first."

The 20-Year Revelation

The conference's final presentation left everyone in stunned silence. Dr. Tan returned to show projections of how these abstract concepts would translate into concrete life paths.

"Let me show you four investor scenarios, all starting from the same basis, and all making monthly investments of $1,000 over 20 years."

A slide appeared:

The Average Investor (Emotionally Reactive):

$493,000 after 20 years.

"This is most people. They try hard, follow tips, chase trends. Fear and greed drive their decisions. They sell during drawdowns, hesitate during recoveries, and miss compounding windows. Two decades of effort for less than half a million."

A second line appeared beneath it.

The Disciplined Investor (Basic Psychological Training):

$912,000 after 20 years.

"Nothing exotic here. Fewer emotional decisions with more consistency. Fewer self-inflicted mistakes. Nearly double the outcome. Not from better investments, but from better behavior."

Another click:

The Optimized Investor (Advanced Psychological Mastery):

$1,647,000 after 20 years.

"This is where psychological optimization begins to reshape returns themselves. Staying invested through volatility. Adding during drawdowns. Letting compounding work. Same contribution. More than triple the result."

The room murmured as the final line appeared.

The Institutional-Level Systematic Investor:

$2,441,000 after 20 years.

"Here, psychology and systems are fully integrated. Decision-making is insulated from emotion. Behavior is consistent across cycles. Compounding is uninterrupted. This is how generational wealth is built."

Dr. Tan let the numbers sit.

"The difference between the average investor and institutional-level execution," she said calmly, "is $1.95 million over 20 years."

She paused.

"Not from picking better assets. Not from timing markets. From eliminating predictable psychological errors and allowing higher effective returns to compound over time."

With a slight smile, Dr. Tan concluded:

"That's the nature of exponential growth. Small behavioral advantages don't compound emotionally, they compound mathematically by changing the return path. Psychology doesn't create the gains. It stops you from destroying them."

After the Applause

Charlie found me after the closing reception, beaming with what looked like paternal pride.

"How do you feel?" he asked.

"Overwhelmed," I admitted. "The implications are staggering. If small behavioral improvements really can create such massive differences..."

"Then everyone should be rich?" Charlie finished. "But they won't be. Because developing psychological mastery requires a rare kind of humility, the willingness to admit that you are inevitably fallible. Most people would rather blame markets, politicians, or bad luck than face their own psychological limitations."

As we walked through the Institute's gardens, the setting sun cast long shadows across meticulously maintained paths. In their uniformity, they perfectly mirrored the systematic approaches we had been discussing.

Charlie paused, looking at the garden. "Mastery isn't about never feeling fear or making a mistake again; it's about becoming a decision-maker who has a system in place for when those feelings inevitably arrive. It's about being smart enough to know you aren't always going to be smart."

"What struck me most," I said, "was the contrast between Jasmin and Michael. Same starting point, different endpoints. All because one had learned to manage their psychology."

Charlie nodded. "That's why I call it psychological arbitrage. The gaps in human behavior are far larger and more persistent than gaps in market pricing. Master psychology, and you have an advantage that compounds forever."

"But it's not just about money," I reflected. "The same set of psychological skills: emotional regulation, long-term thinking, systematic discipline, they improve everything. They're the reason I could stand up in front of that crowd today."

"Now you understand," Charlie smiled. "The compound advantage isn't really about wealth. It is about becoming someone who makes better decisions in every area of life. The wealth is just keeping score."

As we reached the parking lot, Charlie handed me a leather journal. Inside, he had written: *"For tracking your next level of compound improvements. The journey from good to great is shorter than from bad to good, but far more rewarding."*

Chapter 7 Key Takeaways

The Compound Advantage creates exponential wealth differences through small psychological improvements:

1. **Small behavioral changes compound exponentially** - A 2% annual psychological improvement has the potential to create over 50% additional wealth over decades. Small wins today are massive wins tomorrow.

2. **Psychology is the primary determinant of wealth** - Market knowledge matters less than behavioral control. The best analysis is worthless with poor psychological execution.

3. **Improvements accumulate** - Emotional Regulation, Long-Term Perspective, and Systematic Discipline don't just add up, they stack. This "Multi-Factor Alpha" is what creates generational wealth gaps like the $1.3 million difference between Jasmin and Michael.

4. **The 'Fallibility Gap' is your biggest opportunity** - Mastery isn't about being a perfect robot; it's about building a system that accounts for your human flaws. The greatest returns go to those who have the humility to admit they need a system to protect them from themselves.

5. **Changes become permanent through neural rewiring** - Psychological training physically changes the brain. Over time, making the 'rational' decision stops being an exhausting struggle of willpower and becomes an automatic, low-stress response.

6. **The Edge extends to all areas of life** - The same skills that build wealth (discipline, regulation, and long-term thinking) improve   careers and relationships. The scoreboard shows the money, but   the real prize is the person you become.

Your Homework

Begin building your personal compound advantage:

- **Identify Your Highest-Leverage Improvements**: Review the Foundational skills (Emotional Regulation, Long-Term Perspective, Systematic Discipline). Which would create the biggest impact for you? Start there.

- **Track Everything for 30 Days**: Record all your investment decisions, emotional states when making them, and the outcomes. You cannot improve what you do not measure.

- **Calculate Your Personal Compound Potential**: Based on your current behaviors versus optimal psychology, what is your 20-year wealth difference?

- **Create Your Training Plan**: Design a systematic approach to developing one key psychological skill over the next quarter.

- **Find Your Accountability System**: Share your psychological improvement goals with someone who will hold you accountable. Transformation requires witnesses.

Next Lesson: The Mastery Integration

How to synthesize all psychological frameworks into a unified aproach that works automatically under any market conditions...

Charlie reveals the final integration that transforms conscious psychological effort into automatic behavioral discipline, creating a complete system for lifelong wealth building.

"The difference between average and optimized investment psychology is worth nearly $2 million over 20 years on a modest $1,000 monthly investment. But the compound advantage belongs only to those who begin the training."

- Dr. Grace Tan, Director of the Global Institute for Behavioral Finance

CHAPTER 8

THE MASTERY INTEGRATION

*How to Unify All Psychological Frameworks for
Automatic Performance Under Any Market Conditions*

The Test Arrives at 2:47AM

The phone's vibration against my nightstand felt like an earthquake in the darkness. My hand found it automatically, muscle memory from months of middle-of-the-night market vigils. But as the screen lit up with Charlie's name, my heart performed a strange skip, not of panic, but recognition. This was the call we had discussed in theory. The one that would arrive someday, when theory became practice.

"It's happening." Charlie's voice buzzed with an electricity I had never heard before, like a scientist witnessing a once-in-a-lifetime phenomenon. "The integration event we have been building toward. Everything you have learned, every framework we have developed, every psychological skill you have mastered, it's all about to be tested."

I sat up, bare feet finding the cold floor, grounding me instantly. "What's happening?"

"Look at your phone."

Pulling up a pricing chart, the numbers there arrested my next breath. Bitcoin: -47%. Ethereum: -52%. My portfolio value, built carefully over months of systematic investing, had been cut nearly in half while I slept.

"This is the most severe coordination cascade in crypto history," Charlie continued in flat tones. "Complete liquidation panic across every major exchange. Billions in forced selling. Peak fear indicators across all metrics."

For a split second my old self resurfaced. The one who would have been frantically selling, desperately trying to save what's left. I felt him there, like the ghost of panicked decisions past.

Then the training took over.

"Charlie," I said, surprising myself with the steadiness in my voice, "I'm not scared. I am... curious. Is that normal?"

His laugh was pure delight. "That's not normal. That is mastery. Your frameworks are integrating in real-time. Get dressed. You need to see this."

As I pulled some clothes on, my phone erupted with increasingly panicked messages:

- *"ARE YOU SEEING THIS?? CRYPTO IS DEAD!"*

- *"Sold everything. You should too. This is the end."*

- *"My cousin lost his house deposit. GET OUT NOW!!"*

I noticed my response to each message. Every one was met with clinical interest rather than emotional contagion. The fear was data, not a driver.

The Integration Laboratory

Charlie's office at 4AM felt like mission control. On every wall screens blazed with price charts that hemorrhaged red lines and liquidation cascades. Charlie's social sentiment indicators had all reached 'Extreme Fear.'

But it was the people that caught my attention.

Alice sat calmly at a terminal, the same woman who had called me in tears just months ago after panic-trading away two years of gains. Now she looked like a surgeon in an operating room, focused, precise, untouched by the surrounding chaos. Her transformation was visible even in the way she held her coffee cup, steady, unwavering.

Simon stood by the window, watching the city wake up to financial catastrophe. The man who had previously lost everything to leverage now radiated a strange peace. He caught my eye and smiled. "Funny

how different it feels when you're prepared," he said. "Last time, I was the crisis. Now I'm just observing it."

Dr. Webb had sensors and laptops spread across a conference table, turning diffuse but widespread trauma into data. "Perfect timing," he said without looking up. "We are about to witness something remarkable. This is how trained minds respond to maximum stress versus untrained ones."

"Welcome to the integration laboratory," Charlie announced, gestuing toward his command center. "This is where we'll discover whether psychological training creates genuine mastery or just theoretical knowledge."

He pulled up a display showing real-time psychological indicators.

"Look at this," he said. "The entire market is in fight-or-flight mode. Panic selling is up 340%. Stress indicators at highs I've never seen before. But look at our group's readings."

Yet our own metrics sailed on in stark contrast: heart rates barely elevated, decision-making patterns consistent with calm market code-tions, not the tempest we were witnessing. We were operating in a different psychological universe.

"This," Charlie said quietly, "is what we have been building toward."

Hour 1: The Old Patterns Come Calling

As we settled in to monitor the crisis, Charlie guided us through what he called "integration observation." This meant watching our own psychological responses in real-time.

"Tell me what you are experiencing," he said. "Not thinking, experencing."

I closed my eyes, scanning my internal state the way a pilot reviews their instruments. "There's a layer of adrenaline," I reported. "My body knows something significant is happening. But it's... contained. Like thunder in the distance."

Alice agreed. "I can feel my old patterns knocking. That voice is still saying 'Do something! Anything!' But it's muted. Like someone shouting through soundproof glass."

Simon's contribution went deepest: "I keep trying to feel afraid, and I can't. My brain keeps automatically diverting me toward opportunity analysis. It's like trying to see darkness while staring at the sun."

We opened our eyes to see Dr. Webb showing us his screens. "Your brains are truly functioning differently now. Look."

The electrical patterns told the story. Where normal investors showed chaotic storms of neural activity (fear centers blazing, rational regions dark) in the face of financial catastrophe, our brains displayed something else entirely. The fear centers glowed softly, providing information without overwhelming the system. Meanwhile, the rational regions burned bright and steady, processing data with mechanical precision.

"You are not suppressing emotion," Webb explained. "You are integrating it. Fear has become a data input rather than a control system."

My phone buzzed with a text from my brother: *Saw the news. You must be freaking out. Need to talk?*

I stared at the message, realizing I had forgotten that most people would be panicking right now.

In our strange calm bubble, responding systematically to events had become so natural that emotional chaos seemed foreign.

Hour 6: Watching the World Burn

By morning the crisis had evolved from sudden shock to sustained panic. News anchors struggled to maintain a professional composure as they reported the numbers. One reported on live TV, "If you're still holding cryptocurrency, experts advise immediate liquidation to preserve remaining capital."

"Phase two," Charlie announced. "Retail capitulation. This is where fortunes are made or destroyed."

He messaged our group chat a feed of social media posts, consisting of a real-time flood of financial horror:

- *"Lost six years of savings in six hours"*

- *"Wife does not know yet. How do I tell her?"*

- *"Should have listened when everyone said crypto was a scam"*

Each post that would have once triggered my own fear response now registered as a mere datapoint. Market bottoms require maximum despair. We were watching it manufacture itself in real-time.

Alice shared her portfolio on her screen. "I'm down $400,000 from yesterday," she said, voice as steady as if she was reporting the weather. "And my systematic buying program just triggered. Adding positions across the board."

"How does that feel?" Charlie asked, genuinely curious.

Alice paused, examining her physiological signals. "Calm. Mechanical.

Like watching a machine I built, functioning exactly as designed. The numbers are just numbers."

I checked my own positions. The systematic protocols I established months ago were executing flawlessly, rebalancing into fear, taking profits from stable positions to buy crashed assets, maintaining perfect position sizing despite the chaos.

"I need coffee," Simon announced as he turned to the door. "Anyone else?"

The normalcy of the request amid market apocalypse struck me as perfect. We had achieved something beyond emotional control. We had achieved indifference to chaos.

Hour 12: The Mirror Moment

As institutional investors began appearing in the order flows, the smart money was clearly quietly accumulating while retail fled. It was mid-afternoon, and I found myself staring at our group reflection in Charlie's office window. Four people, tired but calm as monks, while behind us screens showed the financial equivalent of a category-five hurricane.

"We look like psychopaths," I said, half-joking.

"No," Charlie corrected. "You look like professionals. This is what mastery looks like. It's not the absence of challenge, because there's always challenge, but the presence of capability despite it."

Dr. Webb pulled me aside to show something on his laptop. "I want you to see how your neural patterns from earlier tonight compare to your baseline from 21 months ago."

The difference was breathtaking. My untrained brain patterns during market stress looked like an electrical storm: chaotic, reactive, overwhelmed. Tonight's chart looked like a Beethoven symphony. It was complex but ordered, with each section playing its part in perfect harmony.

"This isn't temporary," Webb explained. "You have achieved permanent rewiring. Your brain now processes financial stress the same way a trained surgeon would process medical emergencies — with systematic precision rather than emotional over-reaction."

I stared at the patterns, as if seeing mathematical proof of my transformation. The person who panic-sold his first crypto position at a 10% loss no longer existed. In his place stood someone I was still getting to know.

"The fascinating part," Webb continued, "is that this rewiring extends far beyond investing. You have built a new emotional processing system that will apply to any high-stress decision."

My phone rang. My mother, who had presumably seen the news.

"Hi, Mom."

"Oh, thank God you answered! I saw Bitcoin crashed and I know you invest in that stuff. Are you okay? Did you lose money?"

"I'm fine, Mom. I'm at Charlie's office. We're using this as a buying opportunity." By my side, Charlie smiled approvingly.

Silence. Then: "Buying? But it's crashing!"

"That's exactly when you want to buy. When everyone else is selling in fear."

"You sound so calm. Are you sure you're okay?"

I caught my reflection again in the dark window: relaxed posture, slight smile, steady hands holding coffee. "I have never been better, Mom. This is exactly what we trained for."

Hour 18: The Mentoring Moment

As markets began to stabilize and the first green candles appeared on the pricing charts, Charlie gathered us at sunset for what he called a "mastery debrief."

"What you have experienced in this past day-and-a-half represents complete psychological integration. Not individual skills operating separately, but a unified system that responded automatically to extreme conditions."

He pulled up our performance metrics:

- Zero emotional overrides of systematic protocols

- 100% adherence to pre-determined crisis strategies

- Optimal position sizing maintained throughout

- Contrarian accumulation executed at the peak of fear

"But here's what's most remarkable," Charlie continued. "None of you had to think about applying these frameworks. You have prepared for this, so they activated automatically, like an immune system responding to infection."

Alice leaned forward. "That's exactly what it felt like. Like watching someone else trade with my money, except that someone was a perfectly rational version of me."

"Can this be taught?" Simon asked suddenly. "I mean, could we help others develop this?"

Charlie smiled. "That's the next test of mastery. If you can transfer these capabilities to others, it proves the integration is complete and reproducible."

He paused slightly, before adding, "Which is why I have scheduled a workshop for next month. You will be teaching alongside me. The question is: can you help others achieve in months what took you years?"

The weight of that responsibility settled over us. We had been transformed by these frameworks. Now we had the chance, and indeed the obligation, to transform others.

Hour 36: After the Storm

By the next evening, crypto had already recovered by 30% from the lows. Inevitably, those who had sold at the bottom had locked in massive losses. Those who had bought, however, were already in profit. But the real victory was not in the numbers.

Charlie and I stood on his office balcony, watching the city return to its normal rhythms. The crisis had passed, leaving fortunes destroyed and created in its wake.

"How do you feel?" he asked, a question I had become used to him asking me.

I considered the question deeply. "Different. Not powerful, just peaceful. Like I have been protected against my own worst instincts."

"That's the paradox of mastery," Charlie replied. "It doesn't feel like strength. It feels like absence, absence of struggle, and absence of conflict between knowledge and action."

"Will it always work?" I asked. "The integration?"

Charlie was quiet for a moment. "Nothing always works. But what you have built is antifragile, it gets stronger under stress. Each crisis that doesn't break you ultimately makes the system more robust."

He handed me an envelope. Inside was an invitation to speak again at next year's Global Institute for Behavioral Finance Summit. The topic: 'From Panic to Profit: A Case Study in Psychological Transformation.'

Another invitation to present my results but this time, no trembling hands. Just quiet recognition of how far this journey had taken me.

"You have graduated," Charlie said simply. "From student to teacher. From learning about frameworks to living them. From conscious application to unconscious mastery."

I thought about the road from that first panic-driven trade to tonight's systematic execution during chaos. The frameworks had not just changed my investing. They had changed who I was.

"What's next?" I asked.

"Now you help others transform themselves," Charlie said. "It's exponential. Every person you teach who achieves mastery multiplies your impact. Your psychological development becomes a compound advantage that extends way beyond your own wealth."

The Life Integration Discovery

Over the following weeks, I discovered that mastery of investment psychology had quietly transformed every area of my life.

At work, I found myself applying long-term thinking to career decisions. Seeing opportunities strategically where others saw only immediate challenges. Regulating my emotions turned difficult conversations into productive dialogues, just as thinking systematically transformed chaotic projects into executable plans.

In my relationships, the same patience that let me hold investments through volatility helped me weather personal storms. The compound perspective made me invest more in friendships, knowing that small,-consistent efforts would create exponential closeness over time.

Even health decisions reflected the integration. I started to approach fitness like portfolio building. Instead of short bursts of exercise then gaps of self-loathing, I was systematic, consistent, focused on compound gains rather than dramatic transformations.

"This is what I meant by generative mastery," Charlie explained during one of our follow-up sessions. "The frameworks aren't limited to investing. They become your default operating system for any decision involving uncertainty, time, and emotional regulation."

He was right. Yes, I had learned to invest, but I had also trained my entire decision-making apparatus. Every choice was now filtered through frameworks of long-term thinking, systematic execution, and emotional integration. Yet, I was far more efficient than ever before.

Teaching Integration: The Final Test

The workshop arrived faster than expected. Thirty students, each carrying their own mix of hope, fear, and skepticism. Each reminding me of who I was when I first walked into Charlie's office two years ago.

Standing at the front of the room, I felt the ghost of my old imposter syndrome stir. Who was I to teach anyone? Then I remembered: I was someone who had been transformed by these frameworks. My qualification was not perfection, it was transformation.

"Twenty-four months ago," I began, "I panic-sold Bitcoin at a 10% loss. By last month, I was able to systematically accumulate through a 47% crash. The difference was not knowledge or willpower. It was having psychologically integrated the lessons I am about to teach you."

I watched recognition dawn on faces throughout the room. They saw themselves in my story, which meant they could also see themselves in my transformation.

Teaching others revealed layers of mastery I had not known existed. The simple act of explaining emotional regulation helped me understand it more deeply myself. And demonstrating systematic thinking refined my own systems. Every student's faltering breakthrough deepened my own integration.

One student reminded me painfully of myself. Cru was gifted but at the same time emotionally chaotic, knowledgeable but psychologically fragmented. After struggling through the first exercises, he approached me during a break.

"I understand everything intellectually," he began, his frustration evident. "But when I try to apply it, my emotions take over. How do I bridge that gap?"

I remembered asking Charlie the same question at the beginning of my journey. "You don't bridge it," I told him. "You build systems that work regardless of your emotions. The gap between head and heart never fully closes, you just use the system to make the gap irrelevant."

His eyes lit up with understanding. Three weeks later, Cru sent me a message: "Survived my first major correction without panic selling. The system worked exactly like you said. For the first time, I felt like the architect, not the victim."

This was compound advantage in action, my transformation enabling his, just as his would go on to enable others. The framework spreads like a beneficial virus, creating pockets of psychological mastery in a world dominated by emotional chaos.

Watching new students make the same mistakes I once made was both humbling and healing. It reminded me that mastery is not a finish line, it is a cycle of teaching others the lessons you once had to learn the hard way.

Mastery Does not Erase Emotion, It Repurposes It

As I write this chapter, another market crisis is unfolding on my screens. Bitcoin tumbling by 30%, fear indicators flashing red, social media in full panic mode. But I am writing calmly, systematically adding to my positions between drafting paragraphs.

This is mastery. It's not the absence of awareness of the market chaos that surrounds us, but the presence of systematic response despite it. Fear still arrives, but it knocks on my door politely now, delivering information rather than demanding action.

The frameworks Charlie taught me have become invisible, like grammar rules you follow without thinking. Emotional regulation happens automatically. Long-term perspective maintains itself. Risk management operates continuously. And it doesn't require feats of willpower to execute these systems anymore.

But perhaps the greatest gift is peace. The exhausting internal war between knowledge and emotion has ended. In its place is integration: smooth, automatic, sustainable.

I think about everyone still trapped in reactive patterns, destroying wealth through psychological failures and suffering unnecessarily. The frameworks exist. The transformation is possible. But it requires something most will not give, which is the humility to admit you need to change, and the discipline to follow through.

To those reading this, know that mastery is available. Not through trying harder or acquiring more information, but through systematically training your psychological responses. The same brain that sabotages you can be rewired to succeed. The same destructive emotions can be integrated to inform.

The journey from panic to peace, from reaction to response, from knowledge to integration is the most valuable investment you will ever make.

Because in the end, wealth is not really about numbers in an account. It is about having the capacity to make optimal decisions consistently over time. Master that, and wealth becomes an inevitable byproduct.

The markets will crash again. Fear will surge, fortunes will be lost, and panic will reign. But for those who have achieved integration, it will just be another opportunity to deploy their systematic frameworks while others lose themselves to chaos.

This is the compound advantage. This is mastery. This is available to you.

The only question is: Will you begin?

What This Means for You

The next time markets crash (and they will) you will face a choice. React with the masses or respond with mastery. Every emotional and financial storm that arrives at your door is a chance to practice integration until peace becomes your default setting.

The frameworks work. The transformation is real. But only if you commit to the training.

The market will always provide the stress, your new protocols must provide the answer.

Chapter 8 Key Takeaways

The Mastery Integration creates automatic psychological systems that work under any conditions:

1. **Integration transcends individual skills** - True mastery combines separate frameworks into one unified system that operates without conscious effort. You no longer need to apply techniques; you become them.

2. **Crisis reveals authentic integration** - Maximum stress does not test your knowledge, it reveals whether the training you've done has become genuine transformation. Peace during chaos is the ultimate proof.

3. **Mastery operates unconsciously** - Advanced integration means optimal decisions happen automatically. The right response becomes your default, not your aspiration.

4. **Teaching confirms completion** - When you can transfer capabilities to others, you have achieved true integration. Mastery multiplies through teaching.

5. **Psychology transforms everything** - Investment frameworks inevitably improve all areas of life. The same systematic thinking that builds wealth enhances careers, relationships, and well-being.

Your Homework

Test and confirm your psychological integration:

- **Crisis Simulation**: During the next market volatility (even minor), document your automatic responses versus your conscious decisions. What activates without thinking?

- **Integration Inventory**: List decisions you took this week where investment psychology improved non-financial choices. Where else did frameworks activate?

- **Teaching Test**: Explain one psychological framework to someone struggling with emotional investing. Can you transfer the capability?

- **System Refinement**: Identify one area where integration remains incomplete for you. Design specific protocols to achieve automatic execution in that area.

- **Legacy Planning**: Write your vision for generational impact. How will your psychological mastery compound beyond your lifetime?

Integration Checkpoint: The Generational Framework

Six months after the crisis night, Charlie invited our original group for what he called a 'legacy session.'

"You have achieved personal mastery," he began. "Now comes the question of generational impact. How, then, do you ensure these psychological advantages compound beyond your own lifetime?"

He presented a framework that extended decades into the future:

Personal Mastery (Years 1–3) "You have completed this phase. This means integrated frameworks, consistent execution, and proven results under extreme stress."

Family Integration (Years 4–7) "Transfer these capabilities to spouses, children, extended family. Create family cultures that reinforce long-term thinking and systematic decision-making."

Community Impact (Years 8–12) "Scale your teaching, contribute to research, build networks of practitioners who can reinforce optimal behaviors."

Institutional Influence (Years 13+) "Embed psychological frameworks into organizations, influence policy, and leave lasting contributions to human understanding."

"The ultimate goal," Charlie concluded, "isn't just personal wealth. It is evolving human capability to make better decisions under uncertainty. You are no longer just investors, you are carriers of behavioral evolution."

The weight of that vision settled over us. We had started out seeking better returns and discovered something far more profound, the ability to systematically improve human decision-making.

Final Integration: The Complete System

How to synthesize everything into a lifetime practice that continuously builds wealth and wisdom...

Charlie's final revelation awaits: the ultimate framework that transforms psychological mastery into generational advantage, creating compound benefits that could extend far beyond any individual life.

"True mastery is generative, it creates value not just for yourself, but for everyone you influence. Your psychological development becomes a compound advantage that extends far beyond your personal investing."

- Charlie's Final Law of Integrated Mastery

CHAPTER 9

THE COMPLETE SYSTEM

How to Synthesize Everything You've Learned into a Lifetime Practice That Continuously Creates Compound Advantages

The Last Call

I was grinding coffee beans when Charlie called, the mechanical whir drowning out at least the first two rings. Sunday morning, 8:17AM. The time would matter later. Everything about this moment would matter later, though I didn't know it yet.

When I finally heard the phone and saw his name, something in my chest tightened. Charlie never called on Sunday mornings. In over two years of working together, he had maintained his boundaries.

"I have something to tell you," he said, his voice carrying a weight I had never heard before. Not so much sadness, as finality.

I set down the coffee grinder, beans half-ground, the bitter smell hanging in the air.

"I'm retiring from active teaching," he continued. "But before I do, there's something I need to share. Something I have been waiting to give you until I was certain you were ready."

The morning light through my kitchen window seemed to pause, suspending glimmering dust motes in amber rays.

"Charlie, are you...?"

"I'm fine," he interrupted gently. "Better than fine. But 40 years of studying investment psychology has led me to something beyond what we have been teaching. I've been working on a complete system that integrates everything, not just about wealth or investing, but about human potential itself."

He paused, and the audible rustling of papers painted a picture of Charlie in his study surrounded by decades of research.

"Next weekend, I'm holding a final gathering at my mountain retreat. Twelve people who have achieved true psychological mastery. You are one of them. Will you come?"

The weight of the invitation squeezed my chest. This was not just another workshop or training session. This was succession. Legacy. The passing on of something sacred.

"Of course," I heard myself say, I found myself standing perfectly still, my mind racing, not with fear but with a sharp, clear recognition of the moment's gravity.

"Good," Charlie said, and for the first time since I'd known him, his voice cracked slightly. "Because what I'm going to share that day isn't about just building wealth or achieving success. It's about our contribution to humanity."

After we ended our call, I stood in my kitchen for a long time, watching the steam rise from my half-made coffee. The man who had transformed my relationship with money, psychology, and reality itself was preparing to share his final teaching.

And somehow, I had become worthy of receiving it.

The Ascent

The drive to Charlie's mountain retreat took four hours, each mile carrying me further from civilization and deeper into something that felt ancient and essential. Allowing my car's autopilot system to handle the winding roads, I wrestled with questions that had haunted my mind all week. It was the ultimate test of the lessons I'd learned: trusting the machine to handle the variables while I remained the architect of the journey.

Why was Charlie retiring? What was this complete system he had discovered? And why did I feel like I was driving toward a ceremony rather than a seminar?

As the altitude increased, the trees changed from oak to pine, and the air thinned enough to make each breath conscious. By the time I reached the unmarked turnoff Charlie had described, my quotidian world was a distant memory.

The retreat appeared through the trees with fairy-tale quaintness. This was far from the elaborate compound I had expected, a simple wooden structure that seemed to grow from the mountain itself. Smoke rose thinly from a stone chimney. Other cars were already parked in the small clearing, expensive machines that looked incongruous against the raw landscape. Here, high above sea level, the chill burned in my eyes and nostrils.

Charlie met me at the door, and I almost gasped. He looked older, not frail but weathered in the way of someone who had completed a pilgrimage. His eyes, though, burned brighter than ever.

"You made it," he said, clasping my shoulder with surprising strength. "Come. The others are waiting."

The interior was exactly how I had imagined Charlie's ultimate space: floor-to-ceiling bookshelves containing what looked like every significant work on psychology, economics, and human behavior from the last century. My eyes roved over titles on the spines of books I had long aimed to read, while a fire crackled invitingly in the massive stone fireplace. Slightly more forbidding were the chairs arranged in a circle, suggesting a meeting of some gravity was planned.

Jasmin. Simon. Webb. Faces that had been tortured in the crypto storm were now calm and expectant.

Around them sat minds that were new to me: a neuroscientist, a philosopher, even a systems theorist studying civilization itself.

"Welcome to what I'm calling 'The Transmission,'" Charlie said, taking his place by the fire. "What I'm about to share represents the culmination of everything I have learned about human potential. But first, I need to tell you why we are here."

He moved to the bookshelf and pulled out a worn journal, leather binding cracked with age.

"Forty years ago," he began, "I lost everything. Not to markets or leverage, but to my own psychological flaws. I was a successful banker who thought intelligence could overcome emotion. The 1987 crash taught me otherwise. In one day, I lost my fortune, my career, and very nearly my family."

The room was silent except for the fire's whistle and pop.

"But in that destruction, I found my life's question: What would it take for humans to make consistently optimal decisions, not just in relation to markets, but in all aspects of life? That question has driven every study, every framework, and every student I have worked with."

He opened the journal, revealing pages dense with observations, hand-drawn diagrams, and early stages of every framework we had learned with him.

"Today, I'm going to share where that question led me. Not to better trading strategies or improved emotional control, but to a complete system for human psychological evolution."

The Four Layers of Reality

Charlie moved to a large whiteboard I had not previously noticed, which was shrouded by a sheet begging to be removed.

"Traditional psychology," he said, pulling away the cover, "thinks in terms of individual minds only. The complete system, however, thinks in terms of interconnected consciousness evolving across time."

The diagram that appeared took my breath away. It was not just complex, it was beautiful, like a mandala of human potential.

"Reality operates in four layers," Charlie explained, his pointer moving across the design. "Most people live in one. Some are lucky if they touch two. Mastery means operating in all four simultaneously."

He traced each concentric ring with reverence.

"Layer One: Individual Psychology. This is where we are all trying to make better decisions, control our emotions, build wealth. Necessary but insufficient."

"Layer Two: Relational Psychology. Here, your mastery multiplies through others. Family systems improve. Communities transform."

"Layer Three: Institutional Psychology. This refers to organizations that embed psychological frameworks into their DNA. Think Renaissance Florence or Silicon Valley, environments that systematically attract and produce exceptional decision-makers."

"Layer Four: Civilizational Psychology. When enough individuals achieve mastery, humanity's baseline capabilities have the potential to shift. This is evolution."

Dr. Marshall, the neuroscientist, projected images of brain scans onto the wall. "Charlie asked me to study long-term practitioners of the frameworks. What we found changes everything."

"After seven years of practice, you can see that the brain shows fundamentally different architecture. And here is the kicker, these patterns are becoming heritable.

Children of practitioners show similar integration from birth."

The room fell silent as the implications sank in. It dawned on us all that we were not just learning to invest better. We were participating in human evolution.

The Four Pillars

Charlie returned to the board, adding structure to the layers.

"The complete system rests on four pillars," he said. "Master these, and everything else follows."

But instead of listing them in literal terms, he told stories.

"Pillar One: Continuous Optimization. Emma was a trader who thought she had mastered my frameworks. She'd made millions, felt invincible. Then life hit. Her mother's cancer, divorce, market crash, all at once. All of that shattered her mental state."

He paused, letting us feel the weight.

"Emma rebuilt differently. She realized mastery was not a destination but a daily practice. Seven years later, she runs an institute teaching thousands. The daily optimizations Emma makes compound into civilizational impact."

"Pillar Two: Cross-Domain Integration." Charlie pointed to Simon. "Tell them about the divorce mediation."

Simon shifted. "My brother's ugly divorce. I applied our investment frameworks to genuine family conflict. Risk management became emotional safety. Position sizing became time with kids. They are now better parents to their kids apart than they were together."

"Pillar Three: Generational Transfer." Charlie's eyes found mine. "Teaching isn't sharing knowledge. It's discovering you understand something well enough to translate it via coaching into another's reality."

"Pillar Four: Civilizational Contribution." He pulled out a letter. A sovereign pilot program in Northern Europe has already integrated our principles into mandatory education. Fifteen thousand children are learning emotional regulation as a core subject. In three generations, that will shift an entire nation's psychological baseline."

The fire fizzed as we absorbed the scope. This was not self-help. It was help for all humanity.

The Daily Practice

"Theory without practice is philosophy," Charlie said, distributing leather notebooks. "The complete system requires daily integration."

He walked us through his routine with elegant simplicity:

"I wake at 5:30AM, not from discipline but because my body optimized its rhythm years ago to do this. Then I spend 15 minutes reviewing yesterday's decisions. Five minutes connecting today's actions to generational impact. Ten minutes reaching out to someone who could benefit from these frameworks."

"That's it?" Simon asked.

"That's the foundation. The rest happens automatically because I have built environments and relationships that reinforce optimal decisions. The system runs itself."

Dr. Webb nodded slowly. "You have made mastery frictionless."

"Exactly," Charlie confirmed.

"The complete system doesn't require superhuman effort. It requires you to design your life to make optimal decisions inevitable."

The Wealth Transcendence Moment

As the day progressed, something shifted in my understanding. The firelight glimmered on the pages of Charlie's journal, and suddenly I saw it.

"The money was never the point," I said excitedly, the words emerging before I had fully formed the thought.

Every head turned.

"All these frameworks... we thought we were learning them to build wealth. But wealth is just what happens when you optimize decisions everywhere. It's a side effect, not the goal!"

Charlie's eyes gleamed. "Continue."

"Make optimal health decisions, get vitality. Optimal relationship decisions, get love. Optimal career decisions, get impact. Optimal investment decisions, get wealth. But they are all the same skill."

"And when you integrate across all domains simultaneously?"

"You get a life that compounds infinitely. Each area reinforces the others. It's not balance we should seek, it's synthesis."

Charlie moved to the window, gazing at mountains bathed in afternoon light.

"This is why I'm retiring from teaching investment psychology. There is no need to teach investing. We must teach humans how to become fully human."

The Final Teaching

As darkness fell, we gathered around the fire. Charlie was illuminated by it like an ancient sage preparing to pass on sacred knowledge.

"Everything I have taught you points to a single truth," he began, sketching on a fresh board. "Human consciousness is evolving. The challenges we face, climate complexity, global interconnection, and technological acceleration all require capabilities our ancestors didn't need."

The sketch revealed a spiral ascending through time.

"Traditional evolution is too slow. But psychological evolution can happen in single lifetimes. When enough individuals in a population evolve psychologically, the human race evolves with them."

He faced us, firelight dancing across his features.

"You are here because you have demonstrated the capacity to teach others. To embed frameworks into institutions. To raise children with different baselines. You are becoming agents of evolution."

He moved around the circle, addressing each of us by name, before acknowledging our unique contributions.

Finally, he reached me. "And you, with your gift for translating complex frameworks into stories. Your words will carry these ideas to the millions of people I could never reach."

"The complete system isn't mine to give you. It is ours to evolve together. And humanity's to inherit."

The Transmission

Charlie divided the journal into sections, handing us one each.

"My original notebooks. Study the journey, not just the destination. See how messy evolution is. Then make your own mess as you push further from these foundations."

When I received mine, I found his earliest writings on emotional regulation, a man drowning in his own psychological weakness, desperately seeking solid ground.

"There's one more thing," Charlie said, producing a simple piece of paper. "A promise. Not to me, but to the future."

We each signed our commitment to practice, teach, and evolve these frameworks. Charlie fed the paper to the fire.

"Promises written in flame can't be broken. They become part of you."

Descending the Mountain

I left at dawn, driving down as first light painted the peaks rose-gold. In my passenger seat sat Charlie's journal, but the real transmission lived in my bones now.

Three months later, I taught my first complete system workshop. Fifty people seeking investment help discovered they were learning to evolve in the process. The ripples spread exactly as Charlie predicted. Through marriages, organizations, and especially through children who learned frameworks instead of rules.

It wasn't for another three years that I next visited Charlie at the mountain house, where I found him tending a garden with the same precision he once applied to portfolios.

"How does it feel?" I asked. "Watching your life's work evolve beyond you?"

He smiled, hands deep in soil. "Like planting seeds in infinite gardens. Each one grows differently, but they are all reaching for the same sun."

"The complete system," Charlie said, "was never meant to be complete. It's meant to be completing, forever."

The Choice Point

If you have reached these words, you stand where I stood three years ago. Just like that morning when I panic-sold Bitcoin at a 10% loss. My hands shook then as yours do now, coffee bitter, future uncertain. You stand at your own threshold now. But unlike me, you do not have to stumble through years of expensive mistakes. A path exists. The frameworks await. The only variable is your willingness to begin.

The complete system is not complex. Its power lies in compound simplicity:

- Wake tomorrow and ask: How can today's decisions optimize across all domains?

- Before responding, pause: Will this reaction or response serve my generational goals?

- When teaching anyone anything: Am I transferring capabilities or just information?

- While building wealth, remember: Money is just one dimension of total optimization.

Start with 15 minutes each morning. The frameworks will feel awkward initially, like learning a new language. But this language rewires everything else.

Within months, your decisions will improve without effort. Within years, you will struggle to remember who you were before.

But the real transformation is not personal. It is participatory. Every optimization you achieve raises humanity's baseline. You are not just learning to invest better. You are learning to live as a better human.

I closed Charlie's journal for the last time. Outside, the morning birds began their chorus. The same song I missed in my panic three years ago.

Now I heard every note.

My coffee had gone cold, but it tasted like possibility.

The Infinite Game Begins

Charlie was right, this is not about winning. It is about playing at ever-higher levels of capability, consciousness, and contribution.

Your wealth is likely to grow, but that is just keeping score. Your psychology will evolve, but that is just the vehicle. Your life will transform, but that is just the beginning.

The morning I began this journey, trembling and in thrall to crypto prices, I thought I was learning to manage money. Very soon, it transpired I was learning to manage meaning, to create lasting value across every domain of existence.

I extend that same opportunity to you now. Not through my words or Charlie's frameworks, but through your practice, evolution, and contribution to the infinite game we are all playing together.

The only question remaining is the one that changes everything:

Will you begin?

Chapter 9 Key Takeaways

The Complete System creates lifetime compound advantages across all domains:

1. **Individual mastery enables contributions at the civilizational level** - Personal psychological development directly contributes to human evolution. Every optimization you achieve raises our baseline.

2. **Wealth transcends money** - Optimal decision-making creates success across health, relationships, career, and meaning simultaneously. Financial wealth is just one emergent property of integrated mastery.

3. **Cross-domain integration multiplies impact** - The same frameworks that optimize investing optimize every life domain. Master one, master all in time.

4. **Teaching completes the circuit** - Transferring capabilities to others deepens your own mastery while accelerating the collective evolution. Evolution happens through education.

5. **The game is infinite** - There is no final level of mastery, only continuous evolution. Each breakthrough reveals new frontiers of possibility.

Your Lifetime Practice

Begin building your complete system today:

Morning Foundation (15 minutes):

- Review yesterday's decisions across all four domains.

- Identify opportunities for optimization.

- Set integration intentions.

- Connect daily actions to generational impact.

Domain Integration (ongoing):

- Apply investment psychology frameworks to health, relationships, and career decisions.

- Notice how improvements in one area amplify the others.

Teaching Practice (weekly):

- Share one framework with someone who is ready.

- Watch how explaining deepens your understanding.

System Evolution (monthly):

- Identify how your unique experience can improve the frameworks.

- Document innovations for future practitioners.

Generational Perspective (quarterly):

- Assess your contributions to collective psychological evolution.

- Adjust to increase civilizational impact.

The Beginning

This book ends where your journey begins. The frameworks are yours now, not to follow rigidly but to evolve and take them forward. The complete system awaits your contribution.

In Charlie's words: "The psychological capabilities that create investment success enable optimal decision-making across all human experience. When integrated completely and transferred across generations, they become evolution itself."

Your evolution starts with the next decision you make.

The infinite game has already begun.

You are already playing.

The only choice is how consciously you will play from here.

"Human consciousness is evolving. Not metaphorically, literally. Every person who masters these frameworks raises humanity's baseline. You are not just learning to invest better. You are learning to live as a better human."

- Charlie's Ultimate Teaching on the Complete System

CONTINUE THE WORK

Mastery is not a destination. It is a condition maintained through practice.

This book outlines the architecture of *The Mind Money Method*: the CLARITY Protocol, the Three-Layer Firewall, the principles of antifragile positioning. These are not ideas. They are systems. And like all sytems, their value is revealed only under stress.

The real work does not happen while reading. It happens in the moment between a market stimulus and your nervous system's response.

To support that work, a set of implementation tools exists beyond these pages. They are not designed for speed or speculation. They are designed for durability when volatility is highest.

The Neural Audit is a diagnostic that reveals behavioral patterns under pressure, the blind spots most investors only discover after damage is done. It establishes a psychological baseline from which Firewalls can be built.

The Protocol Builder translates frameworks like CLARITY into mechanical decision systems. Written, tested, and ready before emotion enters the equation.

The Implementation Community is a network of practitioners operating under the same standard of discipline.

The market will always provide the stress.

Your protocols must provide the answer.

The work continues at: **www.cryptodecoded.org**

OPERATIONAL DEFINITIONS

PROPRIETARY FRAMEWORKS AND CONCEPTS

Amygdala Override

The neurological state in which the emotional brain (amygdala) takes complete control of decision-making, shutting down access to rational thinking centers. During financial stress, this override causes investors to make survival-based decisions that often destroy wealth.

Antifragile Portfolio

A portfolio construction approach derived from Nassim Nicholas Taleb's philosophy, designed to strengthen during periods of crisis rather than merely survive them. Use a barbell strategy with 80% in stable assets and 20% in asymmetric opportunities.

Barbell Strategy

An investment approach that combines extremely safe assets with high-risk, high-reward opportunities while avoiding the middle ground. The stable end (80%) ensures survival; the speculative end (20%) captures asymmetric upside.

Behavioral Tax

The cumulative cost of psychological mistakes over an investment lifetime. The difference between what an investor earned and what they would have earned with optimal psychological discipline, often measured in millions of dollars over decades.

CLARITY Framework

A seven-step emergency protocol for regaining rational control when stress hijacks the brain. The acronym stands for: Check (physical state), Locate (emotional trigger), Assess (real vs. perceived threat), Reset (nervous system), Investigate (with fresh perspective), Time-Limit (decision), Yield (to predetermined systems).

Clarity Code

The foundational psychological principle underlying the CLARITY Framework: the recognition that perceived threats in cryptocurrency investing are almost always vastly greater than actual threats, and that the brain responds to perceived threats as if they are real.

Compound Advantage

The exponential wealth difference created by small psychological improvements maintained over time. Research suggests that a 2% annual psychological improvement can create over 50% additional wealth over decades.

Decade Covenant

A private collective of investors committed to building generational wealth through patient capital, with commitments to minimum 10-year holding periods, no trading on volatility, and systematic accumulation regardless of market conditions.

Decision Protocols

Written procedures for every conceivable investment scenario, developed during calm periods and executed automatically during stress. Like a pilot's emergency checklist, these require no thinking, just systematic execution.

Discipline Engine

External systems that maintain investment discipline regardless of internal psychological state. Built on five pillars: Environmental Architecture, Decision Protocols, Execution Automation, Feedback Loops, and Continuous Evolution.

Emotional Firewalls

A three-layer psychological defense system designed to prevent emotional hijacking before it happens. Layer 1: Recognition (detecting hijacking), Layer 2: Interruption (breaking patterns), Layer 3: Override (implementing rational responses).

Financial Exoskeleton

External systems and environmental designs that maintain perfect discipline regardless of the investor's internal psychological state, like Iron Man's suit providing capabilities beyond human limitations.

Four Horsemen of Crypto Psychology

The four emotional patterns that destroy more portfolios than all hacks combined: FOMO (Fear of Missing Out), FUD (Fear, Uncertainty, Doubt), Confirmation Bias, and Overconfidence.

Generative Mastery

The stage of psychological development where investment frameworks become the default operating system for all decisions involving uncertainty, time, and emotional regulation, extending benefits far beyond investing.

High-Leverage Improvement Hierarchy

The three foundational psychological skills that create 80% investment advantage: Emotional Regulation Under Stress (+3.5% annually), Long-Term Perspective Maintenance (+2.8% annually), and Systematic Discipline Implementation (+2.1% annually).

Information Diet

A systematic approach to media consumption that protects decision-making quality. Green Zone (nourishing): primary sources, whitepapers, professional analysis. Yellow Zone (occasional): reputable news, educational content. Red Zone (toxic): price predictions, gain/loss screenshots, anonymous tips.

Integration Laboratory

The real-world testing environment where psychological frameworks are validated under maximum stress conditions, proving whether training has created genuine transformation or merely theoretical knowledge.

Mind Money Method

A comprehensive psychological training system for cryptocurrency investors, built on Nobel Prize-winning behavioral finance research. Focuses on mastering the psychology behind investment decisions rather than technical analysis.

Neurological Hijacking

The biochemical process by which stress hormones (cortisol and adrenaline) flood the system and shut down the prefrontal cortex, leaving investors trying to solve complex financial problems with primitive survival instincts.

Neurological Warfare

The internal conflict between the rational mind (which knows what to do) and the emotional brain (which has declared war on the portfolio). This war explains why intelligent investors make catastrophically stupid decisions.

Opportunity Risk

The second level of risk in the Hierarchy of Survival. Poor positioning that prevents capitalizing on market dislocations, being forced to sell when prices are low instead of buying.

Optimization Risk

The third level of risk in the Hierarchy of Survival. Calculated bets that accelerate wealth building without threatening survival or opportunity. Where professional investors operate.

Psychological Arbitrage

The concept that superior psychology creates investment advantages that compound over time, similar to how financial arbitrage exploits price inefficiencies. The gaps in human behavior are larger and more persistent than gaps in market pricing.

Protocol Adherence

The percentage of time an investor follows their predetermined plan even when every instinct screams otherwise. Professional-level adherence (89%+) correlates with significant outperformance.

Survival Risk

The first and most fundamental level of risk in the Hierarchy of Survival. Risking money needed to live or continue investing, the cardinal sin of investing that must be eliminated before any other strategy.

System 1 and System 2

Daniel Kahneman's framework for two modes of thinking: System 1 (the ancient survival brain—fast, intuitive, emotional) and System 2 (the modern analytical brain—slow, deliberate, logical). Investment mistakes often occur when System 1 dominates.

The Complete System

The integration of all psychological frameworks into a unified approach that operates automatically under any market conditions, eventually extending benefits across all life domains and contributing to human psychological evolution.

The Transmission

Charlie's final teaching. The passing of psychological mastery knowledge to students who will continue evolving and spreading the frameworks to future generations.

Three-Layer Firewall Architecture

The defensive structure of Emotional Firewalls: Recognition Protocols (intrusion detection), Interruption Systems (threat containment), and Rational Override (authorized response).

CRYPTOCURRENCY AND BLOCKCHAIN TERMS

Altcoin

Any cryptocurrency other than Bitcoin. Examples include Ethereum, Solana, and Cardano. The term derives from "alternative coin."

Bitcoin (BTC)

The first and largest cryptocurrency by market capitalization, created in 2009 by the pseudonymous Satoshi Nakamoto. Often referred to as "digital gold" due to its store-of-value properties.

Blockchain

A distributed digital ledger that records transactions across many computers in a way that makes the records difficult to alter retroactively. The foundational technology underlying cryptocurrencies.

DeFi (Decentralized Finance)

Financial services built on blockchain technology that operate witout traditional intermediaries like banks. Includes lending protocols, decentralized exchanges, and yield farming.

Ethereum (ETH)

The second-largest cryptocurrency by market capitalization. Unlike Bitcoin, Ethereum is a programmable blockchain that enables smart contracts and decentralized applications (dApps).

Exchange

A platform where cryptocurrencies can be bought, sold, or traded. Can be centralized (like Coinbase or Binance) or decentralized (like Uniswap).

Flash Crash

A sudden, severe market decline that occurs within minutes or hours, often caused by cascading liquidations, algorithmic trading failures, or coordinated selling.

FOMO (Fear of Missing Out)

The anxiety that others are making profits from opportunities you're not participating in. A key psychological driver of impulsive buying decisions during market rallies.

FUD (Fear, Uncertainty, and Doubt)

Negative information or sentiment that causes investors to panic. Can be legitimate concerns or deliberately spread misinformation designed to manipulate markets.

Gas Fees

Transaction fees paid to validators on blockchain networks like Ethereum. These fees can vary significantly based on network congestion.

HODL

Crypto slang meaning to hold onto investments rather than sell, regardless of market volatility. Originally a misspelling of "hold" that became an acronym for "Hold On for Dear Life."

ICO (Initial Coin Offering)

A fundraising method where new cryptocurrency projects sell tokens to early investors. Similar to an IPO in traditional finance but largely unregulated.

Layer 1

The base blockchain protocol (e.g., Bitcoin, Ethereum, Solana) upon which other applications and protocols can be built.

Liquidation

The forced closure of a leveraged position when the value falls below the required margin threshold. Results in automatic selling of assets, often at the worst possible time.

Liquidation Cascade

A chain reaction of forced selling in which liquidations trigger price drops, which trigger more liquidations, creating a self-reinforcing downward spiral.

Market Capitalization (Market Cap)

The total value of a cryptocurrency, calculated by multiplying the current price by the total circulating supply. Used to rank cryptocurrencies by size.

Meme Coin

A cryptocurrency created as a joke or based on internet memes, often lacking fundamental utility. Examples include Dogecoin and Shiba Inu.

Mining

The process of validating transactions and adding them to a blockchain using computational power. Miners are rewarded with newly created cryptocurrency.

NFT (Non-Fungible Token)

A unique digital asset stored on a blockchain that represents ownership of items like art, music, or collectibles.

On-Chain Metrics

Data derived directly from blockchain activity, such as active addresses, transaction volume, and wallet movements. Used for fundamental analysis.

Pump and Dump

A market manipulation scheme where the price is artificially inflated ("pumped") through coordinated buying and hype, then sold off ("dumped") at a profit, leaving later buyers with losses.

Rug Pull

A type of scam where project developers abandon a project and run away with investor funds. Common in the DeFi and NFT space.

Smart Contract

Self-executing code stored on a blockchain that automatically enforces the terms of an agreement when predetermined conditions are met.

Smart Money

Institutional investors or sophisticated individuals whose trading patterns often indicate informed decision-making. Tracking smart money flows can provide insight into market direction.

Solana (SOL)

A high-performance blockchain platform known for fast transaction speeds and low fees. Popular for DeFi applications and NFTs.

Stablecoin

A cryptocurrency designed to maintain a stable value by being pegged to a reserve asset like the US dollar. Examples include USDT (Tether) and USDC.

Tokenomics

The economic structure and incentive mechanisms built into a cryptocurrency, including supply schedules, distribution, and utility.

Wallet

Software or hardware used to store, send, and receive cryptocurrency. Can be "hot" (connected to the internet) or "cold" (offline storage).

Whale

An individual or entity that holds a large amount of cryptocurrency, capable of influencing market prices through large trades.

Whitepaper

A technical document outlining a cryptocurrency project's concept, technology, and roadmap. The Bitcoin whitepaper published in 2008 started the cryptocurrency revolution.

TRADING AND INVESTMENT TERMS

Bear Market

A prolonged period of declining prices, typically defined as a 20% or greater drop from recent highs. Characterized by pessimism and reduced trading activity.

Bull Market

A prolonged period of rising prices, characterized by optimism and increased investor confidence.

Contrarian Analysis

The practice of questioning consensus views and looking for opportunities where the crowd is likely wrong. Professional money makes money by being right when consensus is wrong.

Correction

A short-term price decline of 10–20% from recent highs. A normal part of market cycles that can present buying opportunities.

Dollar-Cost Averaging (DCA)

An investment strategy where a fixed amount is invested at regular intervals regardless of price. Reduces the impact of volatility and removes the need to time the market.

Drawdown

The peak-to-trough decline during a specific period of an investment. A 50% drawdown means the value dropped 50% from its highest point.

Entry Point

The price level at which an investor initiates a position. Optimizing entry points can significantly improve long-term returns.

Exit Strategy

A predetermined plan for selling or reducing a position. Essential for disciplined investing and avoiding emotional decisions.

Leverage

Using borrowed funds to increase the size of an investment position. Amplifies both gains and losses and introduces liquidation risk.

Liquidity

The ease with which an asset can be bought or sold without significantly affecting its price. High liquidity means tight spreads and easy execution.

Margin Call

A broker's demand for additional funds or securities to bring a margin account up to minimum requirements. Failure to meet margin calls results in liquidation.

Moving Average

A technical analysis indicator that smooths price data by calculating the average over a specified period. Common examples include the 50-day and 200-day moving averages.

Portfolio Rebalancing

The process of adjusting portfolio holdings to maintain a desired asset allocation. Typically involves selling outperformers and buying under-performers.

Position Sizing

Determining how much capital to allocate to each investment. Proper position sizing is crucial for risk management and allows for controlled exposure to asymmetric opportunities.

Process Over Outcome

The principle that a good decision that loses money is still a good decision, while a bad decision that makes money is still a bad decision. Focuses on decision quality rather than short-term results.

Resistance

A price level where selling pressure tends to overcome buying pressure, preventing further price increases.

Retail Capitulation

The phase of a market decline when individual investors surrender and sell en masse, often marking the bottom of a downturn and creating buying opportunities for institutional investors.

Revenge Trading

Attempting to recover losses quickly through increasingly risky trades. Often leads to even greater losses and represents a complete breakdown of discipline.

Risk-Adjusted Return

A measure of investment performance that accounts for the level of risk taken to achieve returns. Higher risk-adjusted returns indicate more efficient use of capital.

Stop-Loss

An order to automatically sell an asset when it reaches a specified price, limiting potential losses.

Support

A price level where buying pressure tends to overcome selling presure, preventing further price declines.

Systematic Accumulation

A disciplined approach to building positions over time through regular purchases regardless of price, removing emotion and market timing from the investment process.

Technical Analysis

A method of evaluating investments by analyzing price charts, paterns, and market statistics to forecast future price movements.

Volatility

The degree of variation in an asset's price over time. Cryptocurrecy markets are known for extreme volatility compared to traditional assets.

BEHAVIORAL FINANCE AND PSYCHOLOGY TERMS

Amygdala

The brain region responsible for processing emotions, particularly fear. During stress, the amygdala can trigger fight-or-flight responses that override rational decision-making.

Amygdala Hijack

A term coined by psychologist Daniel Goleman describing when the emotional brain (amygdala) overwhelms the rational brain (prefrontal cortex), leading to impulsive, irrational decisions.

Anchoring Bias

The tendency to rely too heavily on the first piece of information encountered when making decisions. Investors may anchor to purchase prices or previous highs.

Antifragility

A concept developed by Nassim Nicholas Taleb describing systems that gain from disorder, stress, and volatility. The opposite of fragile; beyond merely robust.

Behavioral Finance

The field of study examining how psychological influences and biases affect financial decision-making. Challenges the assumption that investors are rational.

Cognitive Bias

Systematic patterns of deviation from rationality in judgment. Includes numerous biases that affect investment decisions such as confirmation bias, recency bias, and overconfidence.

Confirmation Bias

The tendency to search for, interpret, and recall information that confirms existing beliefs while ignoring contradictory evidence.

Cortisol

A stress hormone released during financial anxiety that impairs memory, reduces access to stored knowledge, and degrades decision-making quality.

Decision Fatigue

The deteriorating quality of decisions made after a long session of decision-making. Explains why investors make worse choices when stressed, tired, or overwhelmed.

Disposition Effect

The tendency for investors to sell winning investments too early while holding losing investments too long. Driven by loss aversion.

Ego Depletion

The idea that self-control draws upon a limited pool of mental resources. As willpower is used, it becomes depleted, making subsequent self-control more difficult.

Emotional Intelligence (EI)

The ability to recognize, understand, and manage one's own emotions and the emotions of others. Crucial for investment success.

Fight-or-Flight Response

The body's automatic physiological reaction to perceived threats, redirecting blood flow from thinking centers to muscles for physical action. Evolutionarily useful for predators, destructive for portfolio management.

Herd Behavior

The tendency to follow and copy what others are doing rather than making independent decisions. Amplifies market bubbles and crashes.

Loss Aversion

A principle from prospect theory stating that losses hurt approximately twice as much as equivalent gains feel good. Leads to irrational risk-seeking to avoid losses.

Mental Accounting

The tendency to categorize and treat money differently depending on its source, intended use, or mental "account." Can lead to irrational financial decisions.

Neural Rewiring

The brain's ability to form new pathways through consistent psychological practice, eventually making optimal decisions automatic rather than requiring conscious effort.

Overconfidence Bias

The tendency to overestimate one's own abilities, knowledge, or the precision of one's predictions. Common after a series of successful investments.

Panic Selling

The emotional decision to sell investments during market stress, typically locking in losses at the worst possible time and often occurring during maximum fear.

Parasympathetic Nervous System

The "rest and digest" system that counteracts stress responses. Activation through specific breathing techniques can restore rational thinking during market panic.

Prefrontal Cortex

The brain region responsible for complex cognitive behavior, decision-making, and moderating social behavior. The "rational brain" that gets overwhelmed during stress.

Probabilistic Thinking

The practice of assigning probabilities to multiple scenarios rather than making binary predictions. Fundamental to professional-grade investment decision-making.

Prospect Theory

A behavioral economic theory developed by Daniel Kahneman and Amos Tversky describing how people make decisions involving risk and uncertainty. Won Kahneman the Nobel Prize in Economics.

Rationalization

The process by which a stressed brain creates elaborate justifications for terrible decisions, making destructive choices feel completely logical in the moment.

Recency Bias

The tendency to weight recent events more heavily than earlier events when making decisions. Leads to extrapolating recent trends into the future.

Regret Aversion

The tendency to avoid actions that might lead to regret, even when those actions are rational. Can cause paralysis in decision-making.

Vagus Nerve

The primary nerve controlling the parasympathetic nervous system. Stimulation through specific breathing techniques can shift brain chemistry from stress mode to calm.

Willpower Paradox

The counterintuitive finding that trying harder to maintain discipline through force of will makes catastrophic failure more likely. Truly disciplined people use less willpower, not more.

FURTHER READING AND RESEARCH SOURCES

The psychological frameworks presented in this book are grounded in decades of peer-reviewed research from Nobel Prize-winning economists, behavioral psychologists, and neuroscientists. Below are the foundational works that informed The Mind Money Method.

Foundational Behavioral Economics

Kahneman, D. (2011). Thinking, Fast and Slow. Farrar, Straus and Giroux.

The definitive work on cognitive biases and decision-making by the Nobel laureate. Introduces System 1 and System 2 thinking and explains how psychological biases systematically affect judgment under uncertainty.

Kahneman, D., & Tversky, A. (1979). Prospect Theory: An Analysis of Decision under Risk. Econometrica, 47(2), 263–291.

The most-cited paper in economics, establishing the foundational theory of loss aversion and how people evaluate gains and losses asymmetrically. Essential reading for understanding investor psychology.

Duhigg, C. (2012). The Power of Habit: Why We Do What We Do in Life and Business. Random House.

Examines the science of habit formation and how automatic behaviors can be intentionally designed. Applicable to building investment routines that operate independently of emotional state.

Investor Psychology and Market Behavior

Shiller, R. J. (2015). Irrational Exuberance (3rd ed.) Princeton University Press.

Nobel laureate Robert Shiller's analysis of speculative bubbles and the psychological forces that drive them. Essential for understanding market cycles and crowd psychology.

Montier, J. (2010). The Little Book of Behavioral Investing: How Not to Be Your Own Worst Enemy. John Wiley & Sons.

Practical guide to recognizing and overcoming the behavioral biases that harm investment returns. Includes actionable strategies for institutional and individual investors.

Zweig, J. (2007). Your Money and Your Brain: How the New Science of Neuroeconomics Can Help Make You Rich. Simon & Schuster.

Explores the neuroscience of financial decision-making, explaining why the brain systematically leads investors astray and how to counteract these tendencies.

Lo, A. W. (2017). Adaptive Markets: Financial Evolution at the Speed of Thought. Princeton University Press.

Proposes a new framework reconciling efficient market theory with behavioral finance. Explains how markets evolve and how investor psychology adapts over time.

Cryptocurrency-Specific Research

Delfabbro, P., King, D. L., & Williams, J. (2021). The Psychology of Cryptocurrency Trading: Risk and Protective Factors. Journal of Behavioral Addictions, 10(2), 201–207.

Peer-reviewed analysis of psychological risk factors specific to crypto-

currency trading, including FOMO, preoccupation, and overconfidence. Identifies protective strategies for retail investors.

Ammous, S. (2018). The Bitcoin Standard: The Decentralized Alternative to Central Banking. Wiley.

Economic analysis of Bitcoin as a monetary technology, providing context for long-term investment thesis beyond speculation.

Burniske, C., & Tatar, J. (2017). Cryptoassets: The Innovative Investor's Guide to Bitcoin and Beyond. McGraw-Hill Education.

Framework for analyzing and valuing cryptocurrencies as a new asset class. Includes portfolio construction principles specific to digital asets.

Long-Term Investing and Compound Growth

Malkiel, B. G. (2019). A Random Walk Down Wall Street (12th ed.). W. W. Norton & Company.

Classic investment guide advocating for passive, long-term investment strategies. Demonstrates why timing markets is futile and patience is rewarded.

Ellis, C. D. (2017). Winning the Loser's Game (7th ed.). McGraw-Hill Education.

Argues that investment success comes from avoiding mistakes rather than making brilliant decisions. Supports the defensive, psychology-focused approach.

Housel, M. (2020). The Psychology of Money: Timeless Lessons on Wealth, Greed, and Happiness. Harriman House.

Explores the behavioral aspects of personal finance through compelling stories. Emphasizes that financial success depends more on behavior than intelligence

Academic Journals and Ongoing Research

For readers interested in following the latest research in behavioral finance and investment psychology:

Journal of Behavioral Finance - Peer-reviewed research on psychological influences in financial markets.

Journal of Behavioral Decision Making - Empirical studies on human judgment and choice.

Review of Behavioral Economics - Theoretical and applied behavioral economics research.

Journal of Economic Psychology - Intersection of psychology and economic behavior.

Behavioral Science & Policy - Application of behavioral insights to real-world challenges.

Note: The psychological frameworks in this book synthesize research from multiple disciplines. Readers are encouraged to explore these primary sources to deepen their understanding of the scientific foundations underlying The Mind Money Method.

ABOUT THE AUTHOR

Casey Cavender entered the crypto market in 2019 and learned a lesson most investors never recover from: knowing what to do is irrelevant if your psychology fails under pressure.

That realization led him beyond charts and narratives into the behavioral finance research behind crypto's persistent 90% failure rate. What he found was not a lack of intelligence or information, but predictable biological responses to uncertainty, volatility, and loss. The same Nobel Prize recognized principles that govern institutional decision-making were quietly working against retail investors who didn't know how to see them.

A John Maxwell certified coach with over two decades of Fortune 500 leadership experience, Casey developed the Mind Money Method™ to bridge the gap between insight and execution. His work focuses on building systematic decision frameworks designed to function precisely when emotion, stress, and volatility peak.

Crypto Decoded documents the psychological architecture required to survive and compound inside the world's most volatile markets.

www.cryptodecoded.org